HIS

A Memoir of Abuse, Forgiveness, and Discovering God's Love

JAYE WIEGOLD

WESTBOW
PRESS®
A DIVISION OF THOMAS NELSON
& ZONDERVAN

Edited by Anna Floit, proprietor of the Peacock Quill, www.ThePeacockQuill.com

WestBow Press books may be ordered through booksellers or by contacting:

WestBow Press
A Division of Thomas Nelson & Zondervan
1663 Liberty Drive
Bloomington, IN 47403
www.westbowpress.com
1 (866) 928-1240

ISBN: 978-1-5127-0040-4 (sc)
ISBN: 978-1-5127-0042-8 (hc)
ISBN: 978-1-5127-0041-1 (e)

Library of Congress Control Number: 2015918380

Print information available on the last page.

WestBow Press rev. date: 12/09/2015

CONTENTS

FOREWORD

I have known Jaye Wiegold since I was a young girl growing up in the church my parents founded. She has been a healing blessing to countless women who have come through its doors—and well beyond—as an instrumental Bible teacher, lay counselor, and now author. Perhaps most endearing to my own heart, she has been a blessing to *me*. Always a phone call or e-mail away, Jaye has been there for me many times over the past several years for encouragement through depression and anxiety, for prayer, and also for insight into some of life's deepest pain. Through it all, she has never failed to point me to Jesus.

As Jaye has proved such an encouragement to me, a dear companion for the journey, I couldn't be happier to offer you her story—the story of how God has healed her into the woman she now is, a transformation so radical it's hard to imagine how broken her life once was. Whether you've experienced the trauma of abuse, divorce, miscarriage, or the task to forgive the seemingly impossible, *His* will be a kind and gentle hand leading you to the Savior—the only place where true healing is possible.

—Kelly Minter, Bible teacher and author of
Nehemiah: A Heart That Can Break

PRELUDE

I was born. That is how my story begins. What has filled the pages between then and now is a story that only the Lord could write—one that only He would choose. He has been good to me as He has orchestrated every chapter, every page, and every word.

This story isn't just my story; it is *His. I am His!*

The narrative of my life began as one of physical and sexual abuse, sadness, fear, depression, desperation, and hopelessness. With Jesus Christ, it became one of love, forgiveness, healing, freedom, and life eternal that began the day I met Him.

The Christian life is not always easy; it certainly hasn't been for me. Even after I became a believer, my relationship with the Lord has been excruciating at times as I've wrestled with questions that still challenge and grow my faith. *Does God really love me? Will I ever be able to trust Him? Is He really powerful— or really good? Is healing from so many years of painful abuse and suffering even possible?* The answer to all of these questions is a resounding *yes!*

The Lord has mercifully used times of hopelessness in my life to draw me closer to Him. In my time alone with Him, He has peeled away many layers of *me* from *me* … and yet there are so many more layers to go. With each one that He strips away, He replaces it with a deeper understanding of who He is and a greater sense of awe for Him and His most amazing grace. Not just His saving grace, but His grace that sustains me in the circumstances of everyday life.

With each shred of flesh that is torn away, He asks a very direct question, one that requires an answer: *Are you in? Are you willing to walk with me?* My prayerful answer is, *Yes, Lord. I am in.* How could it be anything else? How can I not offer my life to Him for His pleasure, purpose, and glory? *He,* after all, is God. How, as His redeemed, can *we* not offer our lives to Him? How could our response be anything else? Our love for Him, and therefore the offering of our lives, is our direct response to His perfect love for us that was proven at Calvary. It is our response to Him for what He has *already done* for us—become the offering for the forgiveness of our sin.

The Lord has been writing His story in my spirit for many years. Now, with His help and for His glory, I am writing it on paper as an intentional act of worship *of Him.* As I do, my heart is virtually exploding with love for Jesus Christ, our most amazing, gracious Lord! He has given me a sense of urgency to share who I know Him to be with you, and to shout from the top of my voice about His love and the genuine hope and healing in our lives that is found in Jesus. Not in the Christian religion. Not in the church. Only in the person of Jesus Christ.

My prayer for you is that as you read about my journey with the Lord, you will see Jesus and become convinced of His passionate love for you in your own pilgrimage with Him. My hope is that the Lord will give you a fresh desire for intimacy, or deeper intimacy with Jesus Christ—a profound love relationship that is rightfully ours as children of the living God. Not in spite of the difficulties of our lives, but because of them, *in* them, because convinced of His love for us, we become His. All for His pleasure and His purpose and His glory.

CHAPTER 1

The Early Years

My tiny heart pounded in my chest. I awoke from a deep sleep, startled and disoriented, to the sound of angry adult voices. I sneaked out of my bed just in time to see my father and a woman I didn't know stumble and fall just inside our front doorway; they were both drunk. My father had brought her home to spend the night with him. My mom was crying and screaming, hysterically demanding the other woman leave at once. As a four-year-old child, I couldn't grasp the significance or the gravity of the offense. It was the *intensity* of the turbulent exchange that frightened me so badly. As I watched quietly from the safety of my hiding place, I saw my father become physically ill. Scared and confused, I quietly retreated to my bed, tucked myself in, and softly cried myself to sleep.

Much of my childhood was filled with similar episodes of violence, physical and sexual abuse, and feelings of never feeling safe, accepted, or loved. Both of my parents were alcoholics. My father abandoned our family shortly after the episode with the other woman, leaving my mom alone, with no income, to raise four children under the age of six. We had no money and no place to live. We were hungry and homeless.

Siblings. From left to right, me, Kim, David
(sitting in Kim's lap) and Debbie.

For two or three years, we lived with different people, in different places, even on porches. My mom still shares how she was constantly fearful that my little brother would wander away from where we slept during the night. I was too young at the time to fully realize the torment she suffered as a young mom, so alone. My mom cried *all the time.* It hurt my insides so much to watch her cry constantly. Somehow, even as a child, I understood that she knew it was her job to care for us, but for some reason, she couldn't. I wanted to help her, to make her less sad, but I didn't know what to do. I believed I was the problem, the reason for all her crying and sadness.

Me, when I was about 5 years old.

When I was six or seven years old, we moved in with a friend of my mom's and her children, doubling the size of our family, now being raised by two moms. My mom's friend also had a problem with alcohol. She was very abusive and a harsh disciplinarian. She believed that children should be "seen and not heard" and that child-rearing is most effective when executed with force and humiliation. Her approach to parenting was cruel and unhealthy, clearly evident in the way she treated me and the other children. Severe punishment for normal childhood behavior was constant, rash, and degrading. It was often executed with all the children together (boys and girls) and often involved the shameful act of removing pieces of our clothing. And even though my mom was usually there, too, she was quiet, seemingly powerless, full of emotion but unresponsive. That really confused me. I understood mothers were supposed to protect their children. Even animal mothers protected their babies, yet my mom did nothing to protect me.

Our two families lived together as one for eight very long and destructive years. Even as a blended family, having a place to live and enough to eat continued to be a real, ongoing challenge. During those eight years, we moved at least seven times, and I attended seven schools. I struggled horribly with the anxiety that goes along with always being the "new girl." I was painfully shy and awkward, quiet and withdrawn. Even as I got older, into my junior high school years, it wasn't unusual for me to cry during the entire school day. Of course, this became more difficult and shameful as I got older. Throughout these years, I constantly battled feelings of overwhelming fear, panic, and anxiety.

In addition to the constant social struggles, academics were also challenging. I had trouble learning and remembering the material I was taught. Concentrating was incredibly difficult, especially if it had anything to do with math or reading, and of course that was back in the days of remedial reading and math groups. I was in both. The other kids teased me a lot for being stupid.

And I believed I *was* stupid. Many times, I didn't even try to do the assigned work. Instead, I claimed the work of the "really smart girl" who sat behind me to be my own. It was easy enough to do. As the completed work was passed forward, I tore off her name, messed up the paper sufficiently (so that it would clearly look like mine), and passed it forward as my own. Looking back, I don't remember ever being asked about it, although it seems to me now the teacher must have known what I was doing. It makes my heart sick, even now, to remember being such a sad little girl and believing I was so stupid—so worthless. Even today, I weep for that little girl.

As a child, I was so starved for affection that I would do things like pull out my eyelashes and put them in my eyes just so I could ask the teacher to help me take them out. Or I would pretend I couldn't tie my shoe, just so the teacher would help me. Once I even scraped my own arm until it bled because I knew the teacher would comfort me. I desperately wanted to be appropriately touched, nurtured, accepted, and loved. I wanted someone to look into my eyes, be kind to me, and care. I needed to know I mattered, because I was certain I didn't matter. And I was told as much on a regular basis by the adults in my life, through the things I was told or the inappropriate things done against me.

Our meals at home consisted mostly of boiled potatoes and onions, French toast made with powdered milk and powdered eggs (with ketchup), butter sandwiches, lettuce sandwiches, tomato sandwiches, cucumber sandwiches, fried bread, and spaghetti. Of course, we ate other things, but these are the foods I remember eating most often. I don't recall feeling deprived in terms of what we had to eat. I just remember always being hungry, which tells me we just didn't have enough. During my elementary school years, I benefited from the free lunch program offered by the county to children from lower-income families. I got my lunch like all the other kids and then just told the cashier my name instead of paying for my meal. This worked well until the other kids noticed I wasn't paying for my lunch. Thus, the teasing ensued. Kids can be so mean. Their words were so hurtful that many days I chose being hungry over being taunted about being poor.

In addition to being underprivileged and believing I was stupid, I was also dirty—literally—because I was physically uncared for. One day I went to school with hair so filthy I actually had a pile of dirt on the top of my head, which I showed to my teacher. She carefully, gently peeled it off for me and cleaned my head with warm, soapy water from the school bathroom. It left my scalp sore and bloody, and at first I felt embarrassed and ashamed, but her kindness and compassion quickly melted my shame, replacing it with a comfort and acceptance I didn't even know existed. Until then, I didn't know what it was like to be treated so tenderly.

Torment and Sadness

For many years as a child, I was tormented night after night by a single recurring nightmare. I dreamed I was being pressed relentlessly into the corner of the room where I slept, until I couldn't move, breathe, or speak. Each time, I woke up sweating, shaking, violently thrashing, and gasping for air. Each experience was terrifying. Of course, every night I was scared to fall asleep. Sometimes my mom would hear me and come into my bedroom to wake me, so the dream would stop, but not every time. There were many times I went to her for comfort but was instead threatened with punishment and sent back to bed.

At the age of ten, I became malnourished. I also developed a serious case of tonsillitis. I was admitted to Jackson Memorial Hospital in Miami, Florida, to have my tonsils removed. Every night, my nightmare returned. These particular nights were more upsetting since I was in an unfamiliar place without my mom.

Being in the hospital was lonely and very frightening. I still remember the terror of waking up during the actual surgery, only to have a horrible-smelling rag that had been doused in ether held against my face. I was so afraid of everything—so shy and afraid to speak. One day I was too frightened to ask permission to use the bathroom, and consequently, I wet my bed. I was incredibly embarrassed when the nurse discovered what I had done and so humiliated when the other children in the ward learned of my disgrace as the nurse changed my sheets. She was unkind, publicly chastising me for being a "baby" and complaining about how busy she was. I cried, adding to my shame. I just wanted my mom.

There are no words to adequately express how much I missed her. I cried for her constantly, but she only visited me once during my weeklong hospital stay. Even then, she didn't actually *enter* the hospital. The nurse came into my room and told me my mom was outside and to look out the window. I made my way to the window and peeked outside; there she was with her friend and the other children. They were all gazing up and waving to me. I loved seeing them all, but I desperately needed my mom's touch. I needed to be able to hear her tell me everything was going to be okay. I was so afraid. I couldn't comprehend in my young mind why my mom wouldn't come to my room to visit me—other than she just didn't want to. All the other sick kids' moms came to see them and even stayed awhile. They even sat on their beds with them. And some of these other kids' moms visited with me, too. They were so kind to do that, but of course, as a sick little girl in a strange place, suffering from having my tonsils removed, I just wanted my mom—my *own* mom—with me.

Other people came to see me too—strangers, authorities— and they asked a lot of questions about my mom. Looking back, I believe they were social workers who worked for the county. I'm not sure why, but for a long time, I endured an instinctive, deep-down fear that one day someone was going to take me away from my mom. And, no matter what, this could not happen—ever. I never wanted to be taken away from her. And I didn't want anyone to think badly of her either. I loved my mom, and the thought of not being with her terrified me.

It turned out that my instincts were right. Sort of. Sometime within the next couple of years, I experienced what was unquestionably the most difficult time of my childhood. My older sister was sent away from our home to live in a different state with a relative. I didn't understand what was happening— only that a decision had been made that it would be best for her to be removed from our home for a period of time. This was the most distressing, disheartening time of my life up until this point because she and I were so close. We were not just sisters; we were very good friends. I longed for her with an unrelenting homesickness. I was afraid that I, too, or even my younger sister or baby brother, would be sent away, especially since I didn't really understand why she had to leave. I was overcome with fear, uncertainty, and depression.

I grieved horribly without my sister, and because of this, my mom arranged for me to visit her for a weekend. At this point, my sister and I had been apart for about six months, so I was extremely excited to see her. However, our visit together proved to be very awkward. We were sisters, but strangers. The life she was living was different—*she* was different—and she loved it. She was enjoying her new school and friends, and it seemed as if she had moved on, but without me. Our visit together was emotionally difficult, just one argument after another. Then, in contrast, saying goodbye at the end of the weekend was agonizing for both of us. We held onto each other so tightly, crying and sobbing, that we actually had to be pulled apart. There was just so much I didn't understand. I was confused and sad, and I was probably mad at her for leaving me, and then for being okay without me. I needed my sister back—the sister she had been before she moved away. I missed her desperately. It was just so hard.

Working Girl

I became a working girl at a young age and held a variety of jobs during my preteen and early teenage years. Every penny I earned went directly into the family money pot under the pretense that one day we would all go on a family vacation to England. We never did. Still, every Thursday I delivered the *Hialeah-Miami Home News.* I hated Thursdays. I didn't mind so much the actual work of delivering papers, but I did mind the fact that every single week I seemed to get lost at different places along the ever-changing paper route. My particular course of delivering and collecting was about five miles away from where I lived. Between constantly getting lost and my route being so far away, it was usually dark by the time I finished delivering the papers and returned home. I also mowed lawns, pulled weeds, cleaned windows, babysat, and did any other thing asked of me, as long as I got paid.

We also did things together as a family to earn money. We collected soda bottles and redeemed them for two cents apiece. We collected newspapers and sold them to a paper recycling plant for a few cents per pound. We had a regular system: the two moms would park our old station wagon at the end of the street, and all of the kids would systematically comb the neighborhoods, going door to door, asking people for their old newspapers. Sometimes people gladly gave their newspapers, and sometimes they threatened to call the police. We never knew what reaction we would encounter, but we knocked on doors and asked anyway.

The two moms also ironed clothes for people. This, too, was something of a family affair, as my younger sister's and my job was to dampen the clothes, roll them up, and put them into plastic bags, where they waited to be ironed.

Next, I worked in a T-shirt screening and flocking factory. For many months, I worked at one end of a folding machine, folding and stacking hundreds of T-shirts per day until I was promoted to be a T-shirt packer. I packed the T-shirts into cartons according to specific orders and made sure they were shipped to the customer. The work was easy, but the hours were long, competing for the time that I needed to do my homework for school.

When I was thirteen or fourteen years old, our blended family split apart, and we became two separate families again. Around this same time, my mom remarried, and she and her new husband arranged for me to begin working illegally at a club in downtown Miami. To her credit, she and her husband both attended my "interview" with me. They saw the environment and understood what would be expected of me in return for an excellent wage—always paid in cash—primarily working the non-alcoholic concession counter. And they determined that my working there would be appropriate. What I don't think they realized or, frankly, ever knew is that the job eventually included other responsibilities—dancing for and entertaining the men who visited the club or who played in the different bands. *I was their show.* Sadly, I began to find purpose there, feeling valued by those who patronized the establishment. My work became an escape from the sad and lonely life I knew outside of the club's walls. And as one might expect, working in this sketchy, male-dominated environment contributed to me becoming involved in activities that a fourteen-year-old girl should not even know exist.

Working there was such a trap for me. I really enjoyed the attention of men, however inappropriate. It felt very much like I was being loved, cared for, and accepted. Of course, now I know that it was not love *or* care that I was experiencing, but at the time, it was the only affection I knew, and I craved it.

I was drinking a lot then; it seemed to make life so much easier, and even helped me enjoy the work at the club. Actually, drinking made many things easier. Things like a lifetime's worth of dealing with the shame of being abused and the consequential disgrace of my own poor decisions. I became sexually active at a very early age. In fact, sorrowfully, I almost don't remember a time in my life of not being sexually active. To be honest, when my sexual behavior became my own sin, there was something inside of me that knew it was wrong. Because of my personal conduct, I remember thinking that I was really bad and that I needed to be punished. So I would hurt myself in various ways, partially relieving some of the feelings of guilt and shame that I lived with, *but it was not ever enough.*

Hopeless

When I was fifteen, I met a boy at school. We dated for two years and were married. This marriage lasted for seven long, difficult years. We were both young and completely unprepared for marriage. The circumstances of my life up until this point had left me a depressed, emotional mess, full of shame from a lifetime of sadness and abuse. Additionally, there were matters inside the marriage that left me feeling even more ashamed and unloved. However, the hardest thing for me during that time wasn't the depression or serious emotional problems and shame; it was suffering three miscarriages. *Three.* All of them were extremely difficult and painful, and for one of them, I even had to go through a short, painful labor to deliver the baby. For another, we were without health insurance, so the doctor recommended that he do a D and C immediately. On the spot. Right there in the office. And that's what he did. *Without any sedation.* The physical and emotional pain was beyond unbearable and proved to be needless, as I subsequently returned to the doctor's office three times in as many days because the bleeding wouldn't stop, and I was eventually admitted to the hospital anyway. Ultimately, in suffering all three miscarriages, I spent several nights in the hospital. Alone. Heartbroken. Hopeless. I desperately wanted and needed these babies to love—and to love me. I already knew I had no value as a person, and losing my precious babies proved to me I had no value as a woman either.

I was in my early twenties by then and I decided that I was done with life. I was completely without hope. In my best way of thinking, the only solution to so much sadness was death. I made the very private decision to take my own life—and I made a plan. I was tired, and I was tired of being tired. I was tired of being afraid. I was tired of being a victim. I was tired of suffering, completely without hope. I wanted to die because I didn't know how to live. I was trapped—a prisoner of my circumstances, past and present, without any possibility of freedom. Nothing was changing, and I did not see where or how anything could change. I spent the next week or so alone in a room, agonizing, wrestling with my decision. I was at the end of myself, so I cried out to God. No, I screamed out to God—several times. I didn't know if God was real, but I knew I needed help. However, nothing seemed to happen—except that I didn't kill myself. As much as I wanted to die, I couldn't do it. Instead, I decided that I needed a divorce. It was the first real decision I ever made for myself, and it was a big one.

And something new was stirring—something unusual. I started thinking there had to be *something better,* but I didn't know what it was or how I would find it. Funny. I had never experienced anything better than the suffering I had always known. I didn't really understand what I was feeling, but it was like something was pushing me, or pulling me; something I could not ignore.

Lonely and Alone

After my divorce, I was very naïve and completely unprepared for life on my own. I felt like I had been thrust into being—barely surviving one day at a time. I was both lonely and alone, just me and my never-ending, destructive, repetitive thoughts. I found a job at a large computer corporation in Fort Lauderdale. After being hired during the initial interview, I was scheduled to report for work on the following Monday. It all happened so fast that it seemed surreal. I had never been hired so easily and effortlessly for a job, ever. I was glad to be employed with the promise of salary and benefits, but deep down inside, I hoped that I would have a bit more time before the job actually began to get used to the idea of working.

For the prior few years, I had been fired—with cause—from every job I had had. The cause? Incapacitating anxiety that manifested itself through my tear ducts: *crying.* The humiliating kind of out-loud crying that I just couldn't stop, even though I realized that I was an adult, that I was in a place of business, and that it was not appropriate. It didn't matter; I couldn't stop the tears, and they would ultimately cost me every job I had until this point. However, this time, as the sole supporter of myself, I didn't have the luxury of being terminated. Working was not optional; I needed the money and the benefits that being employed provided. To say that starting the new job was hard is an understatement.

For the first few months that I worked there, I was plagued with panic attacks, usually two or three a day, each one beginning as a strange sensation that moved up my arms. Each time the sensation started, I would quickly excuse myself and run out of the building to my car in the parking lot. *Most* times, I made it to my car before the full-blown, extremely frightening panic set in, followed by the inevitable sobbing. I would sit in my car and wait, all the while telling myself to stop. Just stop. I did not want to give in to those feelings as I had done so many other times in my life. I determined in my mind that I would not run away. I would not make the panic stop by simply removing its source: the new job. I didn't want to quit this job, and I knew I couldn't. I also realized that I would be faced with the same type of emotional issue no matter where I worked, just as the prior few years of being employed had proven. The problem wasn't the place of employment; the problem was *me*. I was the problem, and I needed this job.

I suffered from these episodes of panic, and even the dreadful anxiety of anticipating them, nearly every day for three or four months. Though I didn't know it at the time, it was God's grace and healing that allowed these dreaded feelings to become less and less debilitating over time until they eventually ended completely. I know now that it wasn't self-determination at all, but the Lord who gave me the strength to stay, the strength I needed to *not* run away from my new job. He gave me His strength, even though I didn't know Him at the time. And I am certain that it was the Lord who provided that particular job because it was there that I met my husband, Mike.

Something Better

I turned down Mike's first invitation to take me out. I wasn't really sure I wanted to go—with him or with anyone else, for that matter. Following my painful marriage and divorce, I had pretty much vowed that I would not be dating anyone again. Ever. Yet, just as I was declining Mike, the most unbelievable words escaped from my mouth: "But you can ask me again if you'd like." *What?* Relationships had certainly proven themselves to be damaging to me, so the best way for me to completely protect my heart from the inevitable hurt to come was to avoid them altogether, which I had done quite nicely for the previous two years. But Mike was persistent, and he did ask again. So out of obligation—I had encouraged him to ask again, after all—I accepted.

Our first date was different from any other I had ever been on. We had dinner at a small restaurant overlooking the Intracoastal Waterway. We spent hours there enjoying our meal and talking together. Then we went for a long walk on the beach, eventually stopping to sit on a bench along the boardwalk, where we just sat and talked. To my surprise, Mike wasn't physically pushy or demanding; he was different, which frankly caused me to wonder why he had asked me out in the first place.

Although I was trying to guard my heart, I actually thought Mike was nice, and I kind of liked him. I was convinced he wasn't really interested and was surprised when he asked me to go out on a second date. Again, he took me to dinner. Then we walked along the beach and eventually sat on the same bench along the boardwalk, again, just to talk. For hours! There didn't seem to be anything we couldn't talk about. He was nice, but again, he didn't really seem to like me very much—at least, according to the standards I was used to—because all he ever wanted to do was to talk to me. We were on our third date when I found out why Mike was different: *he told me about Jesus.*

It was Christmastime in Fort Lauderdale, and we went to see the Christmas boat parade. Mike and I were enjoying Florida's warm winter air, sitting along the Intracoastal Waterway in our shorts and T-shirts. Perfect. The slow-moving boats proudly paraded down the river, boasting their finest Christmas attire. It was a beautiful sight and a perfect evening. I was probably a little friendlier than I needed to be, hoping to be asked on a fourth date, when Mike asked me if I knew anything about God. I responded carefully, not wanting to give the wrong answer, "Of course I do. Everyone knows about God." Then he went on to tell me the gospel message; about Jesus Christ and the forgiveness of sin. I don't remember exactly what Mike said—this was more than thirty-three years ago—but I do remember exactly what I heard: I heard that God loved me, regardless of anything I had ever done wrong in my life. I heard that I was loved, forgiven, and therefore accepted by God Himself, through the blood of Jesus Christ, because of what He did on the cross. I knew instantly that this was the *something better* I had been looking for. I *believed* Mike when he told me about Jesus because he respected me. His life and behavior spoke truth to me; he cared for me and about me; he was different from any man I had ever known. And he still is.

His

It was that night that I became a Christian—a disciple of Jesus Christ! I didn't know anything about doctrine or theology. I didn't have any real understanding of who God was or the severity of my sin. I recognized my sin even as a non-believer, and I was aware of wrong behavior in my life, but I had no understanding about just how imperative God's forgiveness of my sin was in order for me to be in a relationship with Him. Until that night, I had never even considered what it would mean to be in a relationship with God or why it would even matter. However, that night, I understood. That night, I gave my heart to Jesus, the one who had loved me all along. I believed that God loved me and that Jesus died for me. For the first time in my whole life, I knew that I was loved. *Jesus loved me, and I was His.*

"Engaged!"

Mike and I were married in 1981. As a newly married, young in my faith Christian woman, I heard the Holy Spirit begin to teach me about the power of prayer. My wonderful mother-in-law prayed for years that her son would marry a Christian woman. She was praying for me, and she didn't even know me. I absolutely believe that it was the power of her prayers that kept me from taking my own life and kept me thinking that there had to be *something better*. Do you see the power of God? His love for us is profound. Mike and I have been married now for over thirty-two years and have two grown children, Joey and Katie, and we've been additionally blessed with our beautiful daughter-in-law, Nicole, and our precious grandchildren, Ben and Elisabeth. We are overjoyed to know that our children all love the Lord. I am thrilled to be alive. The Lord gave me my life back. No. He gave me a brand-new life! He graciously restored the years that the locusts had eaten away.

I would not be honest, though, if I allowed you to believe that just because I became a Christian, my life became easy. It did not. There was a point in time when I became a Christian, accepting Jesus as my Lord and my Savior—absolutely. However, the healing that needed to take place in my life—and takes place in all of our lives—takes time; it is a continual process.

The Lord has been teaching me for many years now that being a Christian does not mean living a life free of difficulties or suffering. Conversely, it has everything to do with finding intimacy with the Lord God *in* the difficulties and *in* the suffering. We all have trials that God uses to shape each one of us more into His image and likeness as He draws us into a beautiful love relationship with Jesus Christ. All the while, He lovingly deepens our understanding of the power of the gospel as it relates to our everyday lives. We are loved, forgiven and accepted by a Holy God. Profound!

Realizing God's forgiveness has been life-changing in my relationship with the Lord. This fundamental teaching, and its application by the Holy Spirit, has been, and remains, vital, *monumental*, to my personal, daily journey with Jesus. I have discovered that the process of healing follows forgiveness, and as it has taken place, the Lord has slowly and surely filled me with a deep, personal knowledge of Himself and His love for me. He has given me a love for Him that is personal and intimate, beyond my own understanding or capacity to love. He continues to instruct me about the beauty and the power of forgiveness— God's forgiveness of me, and therefore, my forgiveness of others. As a result of both receiving and extending His forgiveness, I am being continually released to know Jesus, deeply and intimately. I have been freed; unhindered to live a life of worship, every day with Jesus in His power, prayerfully reflecting God's glory through the Light of the World, Jesus Christ.

CHAPTER 2

Forgiveness

The Lord spoke to me for the first time about forgiveness, particularly forgiving my mom, about twenty years ago through an interaction with the instructor of a Christian counseling class I was taking at the time. The class was about small-group dynamics, and it was taught support-group style, interactively with about twelve of us sitting together in a circle. Each week, the students in the class took turns being either the focal point of the group (client) or the facilitator (counselor), and we shared honestly about our own personal, very real lives. The instructor was always a part of the circle, listening and sometimes stopping the group dynamics in order to make a teaching point.

This particular week, I was the client. I shared my story of physical and sexual abuse, my anger escalating as I spoke. I even surprised myself at how angry I became as I shared. The instructor listened and decided to stop the process in order to make a teaching point. In all his wisdom, he thought it would be good to stop and talk about my anger—group style. Not my sad life, mind you, or the different ways I had been wronged, but my anger. I had a problem with that, to say the least. I considered my anger to be justified, right, and acceptable, considering the details of my story. He did not. I expected consolation, not confrontation.

I thought, *How dare he? How dare he judge me? How dare he draw conclusions about the feasibility of my anger?* Maybe he didn't understand what I had experienced as a child and as a young adult. Maybe he didn't understand that those who should have loved me didn't. And worse than that, maybe he just didn't get the fact that it was these same people who should have loved and protected me who hurt me. I was just a small, helpless child. Maybe he didn't understand how hard it was for me to even share the details of my story with the group. *Wait a minute! I should not be reprimanded here. I am the* victim! *How dare he speak to me the way that he did, questioning the right to my anger—and in front of the entire class?* By this point, I was openly sobbing. I was frustrated, hurt, and embarrassed. I had exposed the real me and all that I was feeling—only to be confronted. This was a *Christian* counseling class; these people should understand.

After the instructor gave his fifteen-minute dissertation to the class about how our own anger can interfere with our ability to counsel others, the group began to discuss *my anger.* As if I weren't even there. My head filled with raging thoughts, all competing for my voice at the same time; I thought it was going to explode. All I could do was weep.

The small group discussion eventually moved to the topic of forgiveness. With his Bible open, the instructor began to teach about forgiveness. *Forgiveness? Really?* I understood forgiveness to be a good thing, but I also believed that some things were simply *not forgivable.* I suffered quietly through the rest of the session, in agony.

After the class was over, my instructor asked if I would stay for just a moment so that he could talk to me. I agreed reluctantly.

He said, "I just want you to know that I understand. I really do." I looked at him blankly, wondering how he could ever understand my pain. Then for the next few minutes, he shared his own personal story and experience with the Lord. He said that he had grown up on an Indian reservation in North Dakota. His father had been an alcoholic, and for most of his growing-up years, he was physically beaten and sexually abused by him. He talked about the feelings of hopelessness and shame he suffered when he was forced to watch his father beat his mother on a regular basis—especially as he got older and sensed the responsibility of defending her, but realized he was not physically or emotionally strong enough to do so. I anguished with him as he shared his story with me. This man *did* understand my hurt. So why didn't he understand the right I had to my anger?

Then he spoke to me about the gospel—Jesus Christ and the forgiveness of sin—and how he had forgiven his father by extending him the same forgiveness that Jesus had graciously offered him. We talked a little bit more about what he had been teaching to the class and how, through forgiving his father, he had been released by the Lord to live his life free from the control of anger and bitterness. He told me that my lack of forgiveness, according to the Bible, was interfering with my relationship with the Lord. I could tell it was a big deal to him.

He warned me that my choice to not forgive created a separation, *relationally,* between myself and the Lord, even as a believer. He also said that he was certain the Lord would call me into ministry, that He would heal my relationship with my mom and use my story to speak truth into other people's lives. The very idea of what he was saying could not have been any more foreign to me.

I understood about Jesus and the forgiveness of sin. I had been a Christian for about eight years by then. But I didn't understand graciously extending that same forgiveness to anyone else. Or, for that matter, why Jesus would even ask me to. I knew that God forgave my sin through Jesus Christ, but come on, He was God! This was different.

Exhausted and Enlightened

I went home that night feeling exhausted, physically and emotionally. The combination of my own personal hurt being brought to the surface coupled with the anger I felt from the class discussion was almost unbearable. My head was swimming. Even so, I arrived at home that evening with a powerful desire to dive into my Bible to see if what my instructor said was true. Not because I was so holy and wanted to do the right spiritual thing—not at all. I wanted to study the topic of forgiveness for myself so that I could prove this man wrong. I was troubled; there was something convincing in what he shared about his father. He spoke with authority. His words had power. I believed that he had forgiven his father, although when I thought about forgiveness *personally,* as it related to my own life, I couldn't even fathom doing what he did. I did not believe I could forgive my mom. My mind was suspended in the tension between what I believed to be rightful retribution and the threatening possibility of … well … being wrong.

For the next three or four weeks, I asked and asked the Lord to teach me the truth about forgiveness. I read every passage in the Bible that I could find that had anything to do with forgiveness, over and over again, searching and seeking. And as only the Lord would ordain, my pastor *happened* to preach a sermon on bitterness during this very same time. When at first I heard that this was his topic for the week, I wanted to run out of the building. It was all too much. Too much! I was tired of thinking about my bitterness toward my mom. I was tired of feeling as if I had to fight for the feelings of anger and bitterness that were *rightfully mine*. They defined me as a person; I wore them like a badge. Realistically, though, what were the chances that my pastor would tie bitterness to forgiveness? Of course, that is exactly what he did. He taught from the Bible:

"Do not grieve the Holy Spirit of God with whom you were sealed for the day of redemption. Get rid of all bitterness, rage and anger, brawling and slander, along with every form of malice. Be kind and compassionate to one another, forgiving each other, just as in Christ God forgave you" (Ephesians 4:30–32).

I listened in awe, amazed and absolutely aware of the fact that the Lord was speaking to me. Directly to *me*. He was answering my prayer. My counseling instructor had been right. His words had power because he was speaking biblical truth. I left church that morning knowing for certain that the Lord was asking me to forgive my mom.

That afternoon, I prayed. To be honest, I was a bit frightened by the way the Lord spoke to me so directly. I shared honestly with Him, believing that He knew my thoughts anyway. I told Him that it didn't really matter to me if my relationship with my mom was healed or not. I also told Him that I was willing to forgive her because I was certain He was asking me to. I sensed that it was important to the Lord, and it had somehow become important to me too—not that I could have articulated that at the time. Healing forgiveness did take place in my relationship with my mom, but not before the Lord brought my prideful, rebellious, yet *willing*, heart more into alignment with His gracious heart. Not before He brought me to my knees, giving me a richer, deeper understanding of His grace and forgiveness, *for me.* He started to teach me through what could have been a very ordinary task ... opening the mail!

Forgiven

The photographs waiting in the mailbox that day were not exactly the kind of mail regularly delivered to the church. They arrived in a large envelope addressed to the volunteer director of church outreach—who happened to be me. Unsuspectingly, I opened the envelope to find several photographs of a scantily-clad woman posed in provocative positions—a woman who attended our church. This was obviously the sender's idea of a hurtful joke. I gasped loudly as I opened the envelope, drawing the attention of another woman in the office. She was an older woman, someone I highly respected, who had mentored me for the previous two years. She took the pictures from me and, after looking at them herself, proceeded to pass them along to another staff member. The two of them, both of whom I respected tremendously, began to berate the woman for posing for such inappropriate pictures. They said things like, "How could anyone pose for these pictures and then call themselves a Christian?" and "She should be ashamed of herself!" The more they spoke of this young woman, the dirtier and more shameful *I* felt. Their words cut through me like a double-edged sword. My mind raced back to the time in my life when I was involved in the world of modeling, beauty contests, and TV commercials. I had come dangerously close to having similar photos taken of me. Memories of sin against my own body, from many years prior, began to flood my mind. I felt physically ill and left the church office completely undone—an emotional disaster.

As I drove home, I was overcome by a sense of shame and self-loathing, overwhelmed by a painful awareness of both who I was and what I was capable of apart from Jesus. I suddenly realized that all my sin was against God, almighty God, the Creator of the universe. I was convicted about my sin against my own body, specifically. And I was so sorry. So sorry. I didn't know how to be sorry enough. I barely made it through the front door of my house before I fell to the floor, painfully aware of God's presence. At that moment, I experienced God's love in a way I never had before, and in light of His love, I became increasingly aware of the ugliness of my sin. He knew about my sinful past, and yet He loved me. He didn't overlook my sin or excuse it because of a difficult childhood. No, my sin was my sin. He loved me *in my sin!* And He extended complete forgiveness through the blood sacrifice of Jesus Christ. No additional suffering was required of me. There was nothing I needed to do, or could have done, to earn forgiveness or to add to the finished work of Jesus Christ on the cross. Forgiveness was mine, offered to me freely by His grace and accepted fully through my faith, completely undeserved. Knowing that, how could I not forgive my mom? How could I require more of my mom than God required of me? How could I demand that she suffer and pay, when the Lord God Himself didn't ask me to suffer and pay for *my* sin? I could not. I must not be controlled by my pride any longer. I could not accept God's gracious forgiveness for myself and then not extend that same forgiveness to my mom. *Jesus died for my mom's sins, too.*

The Holy Spirit lovingly reminded me of the truthful words from the Bible that my counseling instructor had shared during my class: when we forgive, we extend the same gracious forgiveness to others that we have gladly taken for ourselves. We forgive as we have been forgiven.

Even though at that time in my life, I had already been a Christian for eight or nine years, fully forgiven, on that particular day Jesus' suffering and death for my sin became more personal to me. I almost couldn't bear knowing that *He* had suffered, and *I* was the reason. My understanding of His forgiveness changed from the generic "Jesus suffered and died for the sins of the whole world" to "Jesus suffered and died for *me.*" It was then that God's forgiveness became less academic and more experientially known to me, through a deeper awareness of the cavernous gap that exists between me—and all my glaring sin—and God and His truly amazing grace. I knew God's grace and forgiveness that day, deeply. And, I was changed from the inside out, thankfully determined to keep my face toward Jesus and my back to my sin. I left my time with the Lord that day with a brand-new appreciation for forgiveness and filled with an almost childlike awe and wonder at God and His profound love that He had for me, personally.

Truth

I am so thankful that my counseling instructor cared enough to speak truth into my life. The Lord used his accurate teaching to reveal the truth about forgiveness and to show me that it is not only right to forgive, but that it is easier to forgive than it is not to forgive. When I did not forgive, my spirit was bitter and the Holy Spirit was grieved; not mad, but sad ... *quiet.* The people I was withholding forgiveness from didn't even know—or care—and I was the only one who was suffering.

The Lord also used the kind teacher to show me what it meant to be passionate for Jesus Christ and the truth of the Word. As I heard this man's godly counsel and observed his genuine love for Jesus, the Holy Spirit ignited my own heart with a growing, life-long, passionate love for Jesus Christ.

I am grateful for the numerous godly, Christian counselors who have played an important role in my relationship with Jesus Christ, those who have listened compassionately but then cared enough to teach me the rock-solid truth about Jesus. I have been equally blessed by the Lord's provision of godly mentors: women who have shared their personal journeys of faith with me and who have also discipled me. They have taught me to take my eyes off of myself and to look up to Jesus and only to Jesus. They lovingly demonstrated the importance of knowing the truth of the Bible as well as knowing the Jesus of the Bible, personally and intimately.

As a Christian lay counselor myself, I do not believe that every hurtful event that has occurred in our past needs to be dug up and analyzed, but only those that contribute to ongoing emotional suffering and distress. I am a firm believer that if we have been taught lies about who we are and have consequently developed a destructive belief system, then we are also capable of disregarding the caustic thought patterns and replacing them with the truth of the Bible, with the Holy Spirit helping us.

It is a wonderful thing to acknowledge a hurtful experience from our past, to subsequently forgive the offender, and then to watch and be utterly amazed as the Lord does what only He can do--heal our hearts, our minds, and our emotions.

CHAPTER 3

For If You Forgive …

So, why and how do we forgive? The simple answer is because we have been forgiven—and we forgive as we pray. In the beautiful and familiar passage of Scripture commonly referred to as the Lord's Prayer (Matthew 6), Jesus teaches the disciples many things about living a life of grace in contrast to the law. In verse twelve, He instructs them to pray and ask God, "to forgive us our debts, as we also have forgiven our debtors." Then, in verses fourteen and fifteen, He tells us why forgiving others is so important:

"For if you forgive men when they sin against you, your heavenly Father will also forgive you. But if you do not forgive men of their sins, your Father will not forgive your sins" (Matthew 6:14–15).

I don't know about you, but I think this is a bold prayer to pray: that God should forgive me according to my forgiveness of others. Especially knowing that if I do not, my sin will not be forgiven by God. Context is so important. In teaching the Lord's Prayer, Jesus is speaking to His disciples, to men who already knew and loved Him personally. In these particular verses of the Lord's Prayer, the point of His teaching is that forgiving others is not optional for His disciples; it is imperative. Jesus is speaking in hyperbolic language: language that is exaggerated in order to make a point. In this passage, Jesus is highlighting the law: the high ethical standards and practices that are not opposed to the nature and character of God, but that in fact express the mind of Christ. Jesus is saying that the law needs to be kept, perfectly, to the nth degree, as it relates to all things, including forgiveness. However, we know from reading both the Old and New Testaments that man has never been able to keep the law perfectly. In essence, it is impossible for us to be perfect, accentuating our need for grace—to be wholly forgiven by a Holy God.

As New Testament believers in Jesus Christ as our Lord and Savior, we are no longer subject to the law. The law was satisfied on our behalf through the sacrificial death of Jesus Christ (Romans 8:3–4). All forgiveness took place at the cross through the blood of Jesus Christ. That is where God forgave our sin, once for all, and extended His salvation to all who believe. When we are saved, we are justified; declared not guilty, forgiven by God, and "having believed, marked in Him with a seal, the promised Holy Spirit, Who is a deposit guaranteeing our inheritance until the redemption of those who are God's possession—to the praise of His glory" (Ephesians 1: 13b–14).

In the same way the disciples are taught in the text, we are also instructed that our forgiveness of others is not optional; it is imperative. However, we are told to forgive others *graciously,* just as we have been forgiven; not in order to be forgiven by God, but so that we do not forfeit *intimacy* with Jesus Christ because our sin of unforgiveness grieves Him. When our intimacy with Jesus is broken and the Holy Spirit is grieved, we don't hear from Him clearly.

While we are no longer accountable to the law, Philippians 2:5 *does* exhort us to have the same attitude as Christ Jesus: humble, compassionate, and gracious. We know Jesus' heart on the matter of forgiveness, and we have been given the power to forgive others through the indwelling Holy Spirit. The rationale is this: we can be willing and able to graciously forgive others since we have already accepted God's gracious gift of forgiveness for ourselves.

Forgiving others is ongoing in the life of the believer, just as God's forgiveness is for us. In essence, we are called to forgive those who have wronged us, releasing them from their debt owed to us, incurred through their sin against us, *in the same way* that God has released us of our debt owed to Him, incurred by our sin against Him. *With grace.*

A Picture of Grace

Our conversation was one of excitement. My friend and I were enjoying a cup of tea together at her home, sharing what the Lord had been teaching us in our personal lives. As I spoke, my hands flew up into the air, animated to better express what my heart was saying. Before I knew it, my cup of tea launched skyward from my hands before careening down to the hardwood floor, exploding into a thousand pieces as it landed. My apology escaped from my mouth in the form of a gasp, yet my friend responded graciously, making short work of wiping up the tea. All the while, she kept assuring me that it was okay, not a problem at all. Then she kindly poured me a new cup of tea, our fellowship barely interrupted.

When I broke my friend's teacup, she didn't ask me to reimburse her for its cost. Her response was a picture of grace.

In her graciousness, she forgave me; she released me from the debt I incurred with its breaking. However, the teacup remained broken. No amount of grace could cause the cup to become unbroken. My friend absorbed the cost of the cup herself. True story!

When God forgives us, He releases our debt owed *to* Him as a result of our sin *against* Him. Jesus Christ is the only way to God, and God's forgiveness of us is only possible through Jesus Christ. In the Old Testament, forgiveness of sin was offered through the blood sacrifice of lambs without spot or blemish, repeatedly. The Old Testament system of sacrifice only *covered* sin; it didn't *remove* sin. According to the New Covenant, in the New Testament, the sacrificial death of Jesus Christ satisfied the law, once for all. No other sacrifice will ever be required for the forgiveness of sin. When we are saved, when we become Christians, our sins are removed. Not repaired like my friend's teacup. The teacup can never again become *unbroken*.

Through the blood of Jesus Christ, we are made whole again, new, *unbroken*. This is the *Good News*—the gospel: the death, burial, and resurrection of Jesus Christ. Accepting God's forgiveness and being changed by the gospel results in forgiving others through the power of the same gospel.

When we realize God's love *for* us, proven by His forgiveness *of* us, we cannot help but to love Him in return through our obedience of forgiving others. When we, through the power of the Spirit, turn and graciously extend forgiveness to others, we are released from the sin of unforgiveness, free to hear from the Holy Spirit and to live our lives passionately, in Christ and for God's glory (Ephesians 4:29–32). Failure to forgive others does not result in losing our salvation. It results in breaking our *fellowship* with God, not our *relationship* with God (1 John 1:1–4).

Power in Forgiveness

Forgiving others is something I have personally struggled with at different times in my life. However, I have learned that there is power in forgiveness; I know firsthand that forgiveness is possible, relationships can be healed, and anger and bitterness can give way to peace.

I think there are many of us who share a genuine need and desire to forgive others but are not exactly sure how to go about doing it. It would be so easy—wouldn't it?—if the Bible clearly laid out a comprehensive, step-by-step plan on how to forgive, a method that guaranteed results and relieved us from this taxing, overbearing sin. But of course, it does not; it simply says to forgive.

I have been asked by many women over the years to share how I was able to forgive my mom and then how emotional healing took place. Forgiveness took place in prayer, when I actually verbalized to the Lord, "I forgive," but then also prayed, "Lord, heal my emotions." Forgiving takes a moment; heart-healing happens gradually *as we walk day by day with Jesus.*

Forgiving others is an event, an intentional act of obedience. Healing is a process. Forgiveness is the catalyst that leads to the process of emotional healing. When we do not forgive, we remain bound in the debilitating grip of emotional pain, allowing ourselves to be repeatedly wounded by a wrongdoing that may have happened years prior. When we do forgive the offense, the emotional wounding loses it power over us.

Something noteworthy, however, even paramount, is the fact that counselors do not heal and mentors do not heal and even pastors do not heal. Only the Lord heals. Only the Lord has the *power* to heal.

In my own relationship with the Lord, I don't really know *how* healing has taken place, but I do know *when* it took place: when I spent time alone with Jesus as I prayed and read the Bible and cried and worshiped and questioned and cried some more. This is when the Holy Spirit lovingly, graciously, caused me to understand the truth that had been taught to me by godly counselors and mentors and pastors. He taught me that I am not a victim of my thoughts—that instead, I am the benefactor of a changed heart. The Lord spoke, and as I listened, the Holy Spirit changed my heart, causing me to believe the truth about forgiveness. Privately. Intimately. Lovingly. Profoundly.

After I forgave my mom, the Holy Spirit was less and less grieved, and the Lord, in His grace, *began* to change my perspective about who she was. It was then, as the Lord slowly began to heal my damaged emotions, that I *began* to see her with compassion, understanding that she is just a woman, a wonderful woman who, like me, has also been forgiven and changed by God's grace.

Extending forgiveness to my mom was a defining moment in my relationship with the Lord. It was an Ebenezer of sorts, a monumental occurrence declaring that "Thus far has the LORD helped me" (1 Samuel 7:12). And the Lord *will* help us! He will empower us to forgive others. We need to do our part. We need to just do it!

Just Do It

My husband and I spent part of our honeymoon skiing in northern Wisconsin and the Upper Peninsula of Michigan. I didn't know how to ski; as a matter of fact, I had never seen snow before then, having grown up in south Florida. However, Mike grew up in Chicago, and he loved the snow and was a very good skier, and he was also very good with finances.

He saw *no* reason whatsoever for me to pay for ski lessons when *he* could teach me to ski himself. Let's just get this out of the way right now: I believe the only time a husband can teach his wife to ski is on their honeymoon. He thought it was cute when, in my clumsy frustration I tried to hit him with my poles … a couple of times. And he thought it was adorable that one time when I tried "with the grace of a sea-cow" to recover after being flung from the lift, landed face-first in the snow, and then muttered a few words about my husband's frugality. My husband was very kind.

He was also a good, patient teacher. He skillfully taught me everything I needed to know to ski. He taught me how to hop onto the lift and how to jump off (although he neglected to mention the jumping-off part until we were already on the lift). He taught me how to stand, slide, and turn, and the most important thing: how to stop.

About fifteen minutes into my lesson, he gestured to what appeared to be a large mountain and said to me, "Okay, then, let's go ski." He referred to the mountain as a bunny hill. A *bunny hill?* For the life of me, I couldn't figure out why the gigantic mountain he was pointing to was called the bunny hill when it clearly looked to be the size of Mount Everest. And second of all, I was pretty sure that the nice ski instructor, who only charged twenty dollars for a ski lesson, would never have asked me to do such a foolish thing after only a fifteen-minute lesson. You see, I still didn't know how to ski; there are always new things to learn. At the time, I learned just what I needed to know so that I *could* ski, but I needed to apply that teaching to the act of skiing itself. It was only a matter of doing it.

That's how it is with forgiveness. I believe that we tend to know that we need to forgive; we need to just do it. That said, I also know forgiving others is hard to do. It goes against everything we think and feel and believe, *naturally*. It just seems wrong—doesn't it?—that we, the offended, are directed to forgive the offender. It seems backward somehow. Even worse, forgiving someone for a wrong against us almost feels like we are giving that person a free pass, completely excusing or discounting the hurtful act against us. Not true. Forgiving a wrong doesn't cause the wrong to be right; a wrong that is forgiven is still a wrong. Likewise, forgiving others doesn't relieve them from the *consequences* of their actions but only of the subsequent debt that has been incurred. Consequences come in many forms and sizes, ranging from the less noteworthy to the more significant—including court-imposed penalties, proving that forgiveness and justice are not mutually exclusive. It is evidenced through the gospel that both justice and forgiveness are matters of the utmost importance to God. That is why Jesus had to die. Our sin debt wasn't *excused;* it was *satisfied,* and justice was served, and forgiveness was extended.

The Bible clearly tells us to forgive, because we have been forgiven by the grace that God Himself has extended to us. When we make the decision to forgive, we can be sure that the Holy Spirit will empower us in our obedience, *supernaturally,* because forgiving others is God's will for us.

We know the attitude of Jesus' heart when it comes to forgiveness: humility, compassion, and grace. Not pride. Jesus was the sinless Lamb of God, yet He died a humiliating sinner's death on a cruel Roman cross, perfectly obedient to God the Father. When Jesus was hanging on the cross, He surely could have thought, *You know what, this is too hard. If I am going to do this, I at least want everyone to know that these aren't* my *sins I am dying for. I have not done anything wrong.* Instead of expressing any type of pride, Jesus' words were "Father, forgive them; they know not what they do." He had no pride. Amazing. And here is the most profound part to me: these are the words He spoke as He hung on the cross. In all of His suffering, He wasn't concerned with being unjustly accused. Instead, He had compassion for the crowd, the officials, and even for us. It's almost as though He felt the injury they were doing to their own souls more than the painful wounds they were inflicting on Him. He looked beyond His own pain and suffering out of a concern for their salvation. For *our* salvation. When Jesus cried out to His Father, "Forgive them," He wasn't only talking about the people who were there that day; He was talking about us. And God *did* answer His prayer. Not because Jesus asked Him to, but only through the spilling of His blood. Only because Jesus gave His life for us. Again, profound.

When we refuse to forgive others or to accept God's forgiveness for ourselves, we are really just saying that the sacrificial death of Jesus Christ on the cross, *however acceptable to God,* for the forgiveness of all sin, isn't payment enough for us. We are really just saying that for us, or for someone else, additional suffering and payment is necessary. That is a lie.

The incredible thing about forgiving others is that we, the ones who are doing the forgiving, are the ones who benefit most from our decision to forgive. In our obedience to the Lord, we are freed from the bitter, suffocating, life-taking, self-imposed prison of unforgiveness, and we are released, perfectly poised to let the healing begin.

I spent many years of my life as a Christian woman not accepting God's complete forgiveness for some things from my past, under the illusion that *I just could not forgive myself.* In my prideful, misguided way of thinking, I would not even permit myself to remember these events in my life so that I *could* realize God's forgiveness. However, please hear me when I say that *we don't need to forgive ourselves.* We don't even have the power necessary to forgive ourselves. But Jesus does! The beauty of the truth is we have *already* been forgiven through Him.

Is there something in your own life that until this very moment you have not accepted God's complete forgiveness for? If so, accept it now. Just do it.

If we are Christians and have accepted God's forgiveness for ourselves, how can we not forgive someone else? When we don't forgive, we forfeit the nearness of the Lord to our disobedience. Our reluctance or refusal to forgive limits our intimacy with Jesus. When we forgive, it costs us nothing, except maybe our pride. When God forgave us, it cost Him His Son! God absorbed the cost, and Jesus paid the price. Jesus' death on the cross was an event of incomprehensible magnitude: the coming together of God's passionate love for us and His own law being satisfied through the shedding of blood for the remission of sin. *Jesus' blood and our sin.*

I know from my own life and from several years of counseling women that pride can be a giant obstacle to many things in the life of the believer, one of the biggest being forgiveness. Pride keeps us from realizing our need to be graciously forgiven by a holy God. And it can keep us from extending that same forgiveness to others.

CHAPTER 4

Embarrassed, Yes—
But Full of Pride!

Picture this: several years ago, my mother-in-law, my friend Kay, and I attended a wonderful international mission conference in Spain. As we boarded the plane for our flight home, we realized we were not seated together. We scattered to find our own seats, hoping we could do some seat swapping after takeoff. Traveling halfway around the world, I was prepared for a long flight, but I had no earthly idea just how long a flight this would turn out to be.

The plane was a big one. It was the kind with the long, five-seat cluster of seats in the middle, and that is where I found my seat: in the middle section, on the end next to the aisle. Right away, I could tell something was wrong because there was a woman already sitting in my assigned seat. I glanced at my ticket for clarification, and yes, I was in the correct place. So I asked the woman if she could check her ticket too. I nicely explained that I thought she might be in my seat. Without saying anything to me, she looked up and shook her head *no*.

I thought there was a good chance this woman didn't speak English and couldn't understand what I was saying, so I went and found the flight attendant for some help. I hated to bother her; she looked a bit frazzled with what was a very full flight. She obliged me, and together we hurried—or rather, ran—down the aisle to my seat and to the woman who was sitting in it. The flight attendant looked at both of our tickets and then explained to the other woman that she was in my seat and would have to move to her own seat. She even offered to escort the woman herself. I began to think that if I knew where that seat was, I would just go and sit there myself. Again, the woman looked up and simply shook her head *no*.

I could sense the frustration building in the very busy flight attendant as she gently but firmly took the lady by the arm, saying "Up, up, up," and helped her to her feet. She walked her to what I could see was probably the only empty seat on the plane. As this woman's family watched me have her evicted from my seat, I realized what a very long, awkward flight it would be in their company. Needless to say, I was quite relieved when the ever-growing scene finally wound down and I quietly sank into my seat, trying not to make eye contact with the older man sitting next to me. Maybe her father? Whoever it was, I did my best to avoid him.

Almost as soon as I settled into my seat, I realized something was wrong. Very wrong. I was sinking into something ... wet. The seat was wet. It was so wet that whatever liquid I was sitting in was seeping up the seatbelt. It was soaked. I jumped up to take a look and instinctively rubbed my hand across the seat surface and raised it to my nose. I was horrified to discover that what I had sat in was *not* water ... the woman I had driven away from her family had apparently gone to the bathroom in my seat.

My rear end was so wet that my pants and "long-trip-mandated support hose" were literally dripping. *Now* I understood why the woman did not want to stand up out of her seat. I mean, if I had known what had happened, I would have let her keep it.

Once again, I went to find the flight attendant, who by now did not at all look pleased to see me. I was a little bit embarrassed because I had on dark pants and there was a huge, expanding, wet spot on my rear end and my legs. I apologetically told her about my dilemma and watched the color slowly drain from her face. "Are you sure?" she asked me. "Oh yes," I answered, showing her my very wet and now very cold rear end.

Once the flight attendant saw what had happened she snapped into action. She kindly directed me to what she referred to as a *special place,* turned my back to the wall, and instructed me not to speak to anyone about what had happened. And she asked me if I wouldn't mind waiting for just a moment while she found something else for me to wear. I dutifully stood where and how she asked. I could hear my very curious mother-in-law calling out from several rows back, "Jaye, what is wrong? Is there a problem?" Yes. There was a problem. But I wasn't going to share what had happened over the many rows of people listening, so I motioned to her to *ssshhhhh!*

The flight attendant called for the assistance of her counterpart, Niles, over the intercom. And Niles responded, over the intercom: "Is this an emergency?" He commented on how busy he was. The flight attendant replied, "Yes, Niles, this is an emergency." I was mortified. By now, the people were standing in the aisles, straining to get a glimpse of this *urgent situation.* This is about when I started to laugh. Awkwardly. It was a kind of nervous, I-am-so-embarrassed-and-so-mortified-that-I-just-need-to-get-off-this-plane kind of laugh.

Niles quickly made his way over, and after their brief consultation together, the flight attendant excused herself to the back of the aircraft, only to return with rubber gloves up to her elbows and carrying a giant plastic bag. She quickly and efficiently removed the wet cushion from my seat and stuffed it into the bag—all while under the curious scrutiny of my fellow passengers. When she finished, the flight attendant made yet another announcement over the intercom: The flight would be delayed another twenty minutes because of a problem in the cabin. There I was, *the problem in the cabin,* still standing with my back to the wall. The flight attendant brought me what she called runnies: a two-piece gray suit made of lightweight, flimsy cotton. The runnies were about four sizes too wide and about four inches too short for my shape and size. The flight attendant explained to me that the flight needed to take off and that the pilots were just waiting for me to change my clothes and take my seat, which had been upgraded to business class for any inconvenience or discomfort this incident may have caused me!

Before I even had a chance to walk away, I heard a man from several rows back yell to the flight attendant, "If she isn't going to sit there, can I have her seat?" She answered back—loudly—"That would be fine, sir, but please bring your seat cushion with you." Wonderful. Filled with shame, I left my spot at the wall and made the long journey forward to the business class bathroom, painfully aware of the growing, glaring wet spot on my rear end and highly sensing the unjust accusation that did not belong to me. Good grief! You know that everyone on that plane thought that I had wet the seat. Of course they did. But (no pun intended) I hadn't. And since so much information about this disturbing incident had already been shared over the intercom, I thought it was only fair that I be given an opportunity to clarify this with the other passengers. *I did not wet the seat!*

I was self-conscious; my dignity was hanging by a thread. I was prideful, embarrassed, and humiliated.

I felt sorry for the other woman; I'm sure she was embarrassed too. Of course she was. In hindsight, I wish I could have spoken to her, but at that time, I was thinking only about myself—about the shame that I felt and the disgrace that I had accepted, vicariously. Moreover, I was majorly concerned about what the other passengers were thinking of me. My desire to tell my fellow travelers that it wasn't me who wet the seat was my focus. It was a pride issue on my part, for sure. I didn't humble myself—*I was humiliated.* And as humiliated as I was, my only recourse would have been to point an accusing finger at the woman who sat in the seat before I did. I'm glad now that the Lord didn't provide an opportunity for me to speak up in my own defense. Sometimes I scare myself when I realize what I am capable of and how *prideful* my thinking can be apart from Him.

The Greek word for pride means *puffed up; arrogant* (1 Corinthians 8:1). When I think about the term *puffed up,* I think of a cat who puffs up her fur when another cat comes along. She makes herself look more substantial—superior—hoping to prove to the other cat that she is bigger and better. In reality, she only looks bigger because her fur is puffed up. Nothing else has changed. She is still the same cat she was before the intruder arrived on the scene.

In the same way, pride causes us to believe we are bigger and better than we are and to become inflated with self-importance and superiority, *self-righteous.* It blinds us to our sin and our need for God, and consequently, to His forgiveness through Jesus Christ. Prideful thinking skews our understanding of who we are apart from God, causing us to believe that He is pleased with us because of our inherent goodness (Ephesians 2:8–9; Romans

3:10). It can wrongly cause us to believe that there is no reason to have God in our lives and therefore no room in our hearts for Him (Psalm 10:4). Our pride can keep us from knowing the love of God through Jesus Christ and acknowledging Him as our Lord and Savior.

The Pharisee, the Sinner, and Jesus

There is a story in the Bible that contrasts self-righteous pride with forgiveness through Jesus Christ and then illustrates how knowing Jesus' forgiveness relates to our passionate love for Him. This account is found in Luke 7:36–50.

There are three main characters in the story: the Pharisee, Jesus, and a woman who had lived a sinful life, according to the Scriptures. The story is a narrative: a framework of events that expose the relationship between the characters as they unfold chronologically. As I read this beautiful story, I can almost picture myself right there in the room with them, holding on to every word that Jesus speaks. He is teaching that the forgiveness He offers is His response to our sin, and that our love for Him is our response to His forgiveness. His forgiveness is the reason for our passion.

The scene opens with Jesus eating dinner with a Pharisee who has invited Him to his home. It was customary at this time for dinner guests to lie on their sides in a reclining position and eat with their heads nearest to the tables and their feet extended out behind them. This is how we find Jesus in this passage.

"Now one of the Pharisees invited Jesus to have dinner with Him, so He went to the Pharisee's house and reclined at the table" (Luke 7:36).

A *Pharisee* was a member of an ancient Jewish sect, distinguished by strict observance of the traditional and written law. He boasted perfection, having pretenses of superior spirituality, speaking and behaving in a manner to create a false appearance of elevated importance and self-worth. He was self-righteous, commonly viewed by others as very religious and culturally elite. He was *puffed up.*

Prior to the dinner that Jesus was attending, the Pharisees had observed Him spending time with gluttons and drunkards, and they had accused Him of *being* a glutton and a drunkard, as well as a friend of tax collectors and sinners (Luke 7:34). Tax collectors were seen as sinners of the worst kind because of their greed and the harsh, deceptive ways in which they did their work. The Pharisees were right in their observation: Jesus *was* spending time with sinners, but sadly, what they didn't see was that He was also spending time with the religious sinner—the Pharisee—who couldn't see his own flawed judgment. Jesus loved the gluttons and the drunkards, the tax collectors and the Pharisees. *He loved all the sinners.*

As the story unfolds, "A woman who had lived a sinful life in that town learned that Jesus was eating at the Pharisee's house, so she brought an alabaster jar of perfume [and went to him]. And as she stood behind Him at His feet weeping, she began to wet His feet with her tears. Then she wiped them with her hair, kissed them and poured perfume on them" (Luke 7:37–38).

Apart from her being a "sinful woman," entering the home of the Pharisee as an uninvited guest was not all that unusual. Protocol allowed for the public at large to go into the homes of others if an important rabbi was teaching there. It was customary for uninvited spectators to sit quietly along the perimeter of the room and listen to what was being taught or discussed.

Envision this with me: The room is full. There is a large table in the middle with several men reclining next to it: the Pharisees and Jesus. There are probably many *men* lining the walls listening to the conversation that is taking place, since it was not culturally acceptable for a woman to sit directly under the teaching of a rabbi. Then, to everyone's surprise, in walks this woman. She sees Jesus and becomes undone in His presence. She knows Him, personally. She stands behind Him weeping, her tears pouring like rain, wetting His feet. Then she kneels down and loosens her hair, which would have been pinned up according to custom, and uses it to wipe her tears from His feet (even though it would have been considered disgraceful for her to loosen her hair in public). As she kneels down behind Him, she further loses herself to Him, kissing His feet affectionately and unashamedly, and pours the contents of the alabaster jar on them, the perfume that she brought with her intentionally, for Jesus.

Amazing! She loved Jesus with reckless abandon—eyes fixed on Him, unaware of who might have been watching or what they might have been thinking. She was consumed with Jesus; it was obvious that He was the object of her passion. She was *His*. She loved Jesus openly, using all of the elements that would have been a part of her former lifestyle, *her former identity,* and shame: her kisses, her caresses, her hair, and her tears. She had been redeemed, every part of her. She loved Jesus with her whole self. As she did, she served Him, cleaning the dust from His feet and anointing Him with oil—the basic courtesies of the day that were not extended to Jesus by the Pharisee as He entered his home to dine with him.

So much can be said about the response of the woman in the story: the reverent position of her body; her weeping tears of sorrow and joy, thankfulness, perhaps tears of repentance; her posture of surrender and worship; such a beautiful outpouring of passionate love. This woman would never need to return to her former life ever again. She was free. She knew the love and acceptance of the Savior through His forgiveness that would forever unite her to Him. She would never have to look for love again.

"When the Pharisee who had invited Him saw this, he said to himself, 'If this man were a prophet, he would know who is touching Him and what kind of a woman she is—that she is a sinner'" (Luke 7:39).

And then comes one of my favorite parts of the text: although the Pharisee was speaking to himself, in his own mind, Jesus answered him.

"'Simon, I have something to tell you. Two men owed money to a certain moneylender. One owed him five hundred denarii and the other fifty. Neither of them had the money to pay him back. Now which of them will love him more?' Simon replied, 'I suppose the one who had the bigger debt cancelled.' 'You have judged correctly,' Jesus said" (Luke 7:40–43).

Both of the men are completely forgiven by the moneylender. The amount of the debt was inconsequential in terms of forgiveness. Neither of them had the ability to pay the debt owed; *both were insolvent. And both were forgiven the debt in full.*

The text isn't saying that the greater our sin, the greater our forgiveness and therefore the greater our capacity to love. Our passionate love for Jesus doesn't result from deep sin. It is our response to knowing and believing we are forgiven—deeply and completely.

According to the text, by Simon's own admission, he believed that the one who owed the most would naturally be the one who would love Jesus most. That makes sense, doesn't it? The problem, however, is that Simon didn't consider himself to be in debt as a sinner. He didn't consider himself a sinner at all. But of course he was. He was a Pharisee—puffed up, filled with the sin of pride, blinded by the distorted estimation of himself and his superior spirituality. God hates pride; this is evident in Scripture (James 4:6–7, 10, and 1 John 2:16).

Self-righteous pride is a sin of the most dangerous order because it is camouflaged by our assumed relative goodness. In all of Simon's artificial perfection, he had no need for forgiveness. And there he sat, in his own mind, perfectly religious, filled with perfect knowledge of the Scriptures and therefore with little need for forgiveness. Consequently, he had little love for Jesus. There he sat, a sinner, *unforgiven.*

The woman, however, had an accurate perception of who she was in her sin and her need for a savior. She knew that she was loved, forgiven, and accepted by the Messiah, and she loved much. There she was: a sinner, *forgiven.*

Inability to Pay

The penalty of sin is death. We are all insolvent; no one has the ability to pay for his own sin. We all sin, and we all need forgiveness for our sin. Jesus didn't have to spend more time suffering on the cross for some and less for others based on their respective sin. The value of the work Jesus did on the cross is the same for all of us, no matter how much we have sinned or how little, whether our sin is less apparent, like pride, or more apparent, like prostitution.

"All have sinned and fallen short of the glory of God" (Romans 3:23).

The Bible says if we have committed *one sin,* we are separated from God forever.

"Whoever keeps the whole law and yet stumbles at just one point is guilty of breaking all of it" (James 2:10).

It is a dangerous thing to believe we are relatively good by comparing ourselves to others instead of comparing ourselves to Jesus, the perfect Son of God. If we claim to be without sin, we deceive ourselves, and the truth is not in us (1 John 1:8). Or if we believe that our sin *isn't that bad,* we will have little or no appreciation for forgiveness and little or no love for Jesus.

"Then Jesus turned toward the woman … and said to Simon, 'Do you see this woman? I came into your house. You did not give me any water for my feet, but she wet my feet with her tears and wiped them with her hair. You did not give me a kiss, but this woman, from the time I entered has not stopped kissing my feet. You did not put oil on my head, but she has poured perfume on my feet. Therefore, I tell you, her many sins have been forgiven—for she loved much. But he who has been forgiven little, loves little'" (Luke 7:44–47).

Do you see what Jesus did? He turned to the woman, but spoke to Simon. Don't you love that? When Jesus turned and spoke to her, everyone in the room turned and looked at her too. Jesus publicly expressed His love for her, facing her, acknowledging His love and acceptance of her. She belonged to Him, she was *His,* and they both knew it.

"Then Jesus said to her, 'Your sins are forgiven. Your faith has saved you; go in peace'" (Luke 7:48, 50).

Jesus told her that her sins *remain* forgiven and to go in peace. The encounter this woman had with Jesus was not when she came to know Him personally. In verse 47, when Jesus says, "her many sins *have been* forgiven," the term *have been* is spoken in the perfect tense, meaning that forgiveness was something that happened in the past that has continuing effect. Her sins had already been forgiven and remained forgiven. She was changed, a new creature, no longer living her old life, now covered by the righteousness of Christ. Compelled by Jesus' love for her, she loved Him with her whole life.

Her guilt and shame were gone, and she was instead consumed with different desires. Her focus was on Jesus, not on herself. Her pride did not keep her from going to see Jesus and loving Him openly, knowing that her reputation preceded her. Jesus wasn't just in first place in her heart; he had all of it! She was loosed by Jesus' love for her and consumed with her love for Him. Forgiveness was the cause of her love. Her love was the effect of His forgiveness. Her many sins had been forgiven—for she loved much. And she worshiped Him.

Belonging to Jesus

When I read this remarkable story, I can't help but think that I want to be this woman. I want to love Jesus Christ with reckless abandon, with *first love,* passionately, with my whole life, no matter who is watching. I want to be *in love* with Him! And I am not alone. For the past twenty years or so, I have spoken to countless women in mentoring, counseling, or teaching relationships who have expressed the same desire. So, what did this amazing woman know that we do not know? What truth was she absolutely convinced of and affected by? She knew and believed that she was loved by Jesus, therefore forgiven and completely accepted, even though the payment itself for *her* sin had not yet been made, because Jesus had not yet died. She found her identity in Christ, abandoning herself to Him for the world to see.

She loved Jesus out loud, with her life, regardless of who was watching. Her doctrine was perfect; she knew who she was in her sin, and she realized that Jesus was her Lord and Savior. This beautiful woman was not at all concerned with her spiritual persona. Her love for Jesus usurped any need she may have had to protect her spiritual good looks or her reputation. It is obvious by her response to seeing Jesus that religion was the furthest thing from her mind. Her love for Him was real. Through her actions, it was apparent that she was more concerned with loving Jesus than attempting to impress anyone with what she knew about doctrine. The Pharisees who watched her were incorrect in their doctrine. They knew a lot about religion. They were, in fact, religious experts. But they did not believe that Jesus was the Son of God, the Lord, and the Savior of the world. The woman knew and loved Jesus, intimately and passionately. Compelled by Jesus' love for her, her outward appearance reflected her inward love—in the form of worship! And so must ours as we walk, *every day, with Jesus.*

CHAPTER 5

Divine Purpose

Uniformed guards with guns patrolled both sides of the border. It was late, about eleven o'clock p.m., and the line waiting for permission to cross from one European country into the next was many cars long. I was traveling with a group of about ten people. Our hired driver turned off the engine of our van to save petrol, and together we pushed it forward as the vehicles progressed. It was a slow, tedious process.

Our instructions for the border crossing were simple: no speaking unless we were spoken to. Our driver went out of his way to say that crossing the border was serious business and that it wasn't the time for careless attitudes. He was clearly intimidated by the process.

When we finally pushed the van up to the guard house, our passports were collected, processed through the computer, and then returned to everyone in the van, except for mine. There seemed to be a problem with my documents.

After a few apprehensive moments of intense conversation among the border official, our driver, and me, the problem was resolved, and my passport was returned to me as well. The guard finally motioned us through the raised barricade into the neighboring country, where the process of checking passports began again.

This anxiety and tension at the border crossing surprised me very much because both countries were free. There had been a time in their history when they had been controlled by the Communist government, but not anymore. It was interesting to me that the people (at least at the border) seemed to be choosing to live their lives bound to the oppressive rule and laws that no longer applied to them as a free nation. They were free, but not living free.

I think the same thing can sometimes be said of us as Christians, disciples of Jesus Christ. We don't enjoy the freedom that has been purchased for us through the gospel: through the perfect life, death, burial, and resurrection of Jesus Christ. Even as His followers, we can continue to live quite passively, bound to the law of sin and death (Romans 8:2). We do this even though through the cross we have been released from both the penalty and the power of sin in our lives, through the burial we have been saved from spiritual death, through the resurrection we have been given life in Christ, and through the coming of the indwelling Holy Spirit we have been given the power to live the life of freedom that Jesus asks of us today. Our freedom has purpose—*divine purpose.* We have been saved by grace, set free from the bondage of sin, *redeemed,* so that we can worship the one true God.

A Life of Worship

Paul described New Testament worship perfectly in His epistle to the Romans. In the first eleven chapters, he presents an inarguable, solid case for the gospel as the motivation to worship.

And then he speaks to the manner of worship as he virtually explodes with his passionate exhortation in chapter twelve:

"Therefore, I urge you, brothers, in view of God's mercy, to offer your bodies as living sacrifices, holy and pleasing to God—this is your spiritual act of worship" (Romans 12:1).

The word *worship* in this verse is the Greek word *latreia,* meaning *the service to and the worship of God.* It is similar in meaning to the Hebrew word *abad,* which Moses used in the Old Testament book of Exodus each time he appealed to the pharaoh, saying, "The LORD, the God of the Hebrews, has sent me to say to you: Let my people go, so that they may worship *[abad]* me." Through Moses, God freed the Hebrew people from the yoke of bondage imposed on them by the pharaoh so that they could worship Him. More significantly, through Jesus Christ, God delivered us, His disciples, from the bondage of sin so that *we* could worship Him. We have been freed from sin's mastery over us so that we can worship the living God—not through the offering of dead animals laid on the altar, as we see in the Old Testament, but through the offering of our living, breathing lives. No more blood-letting is required for sin; Jesus' blood was sufficient through the glorious gospel.

That is, in fact, the reason for Paul's outburst of excitement in Romans, chapter twelve: the gospel! Paul says, in light of God's incredible mercy, in light of the truth of the gospel, in light of the previous three hundred and fifteen verses of Romans (I counted them), in light of who we are in Christ and what we enjoy because of Him, "I *urge you.*" Urging is the language of grace. Not the law. Paul is appealing to our minds in his beseeching—the divine provision of our ability to reason. That makes sense, though, doesn't it? There is nothing in the Bible that suggests that we should check our brains in at the front door of the church just because we are Christians. So, think about what Paul is saying. He is petitioning us to exercise our God-given ability to think and to reason, taking into account *all* the facts that have been accurately and thoroughly laid out in the first eleven chapters of Romans, and then to conclude what he has concluded: the only reasonable response to the gospel is to freely offer our bodies as living sacrifices, holy and pleasing to God, as our spiritual act of worship.

Worship is the whole life response to God for what He has already done for us, completely, through the gospel of Jesus Christ.

The deeper our understanding of what God did for us through the person of Jesus Christ, the greater our desire will be to worship Him.

The greater our awareness of the infinite gulf that exists between us—and all of our glaring sin—and God and His unparalleled mercy and grace for us through the gospel, the greater our need will be to worship Him with all of who we are.

Worship requires the humble surrender of our will. When we submit our will to God, deferring to His will for us, our whole being—our hearts, souls, and minds—follow suit. Surrender is the decision of our innermost being, *our hearts,* a choice to offer God the right to our lives. We decide daily (beginning at the time of our salvation), and then the Holy Spirit empowers us in our decision. The yielding of our hearts position us to submit our whole lives with reckless abandon to the supreme person of the Lord Jesus Christ, acknowledging that He is the self-existing Creator of the universe, the sovereign, most high God. *And we are not.*

If our surrender to Jesus is the outgrowth of obligation or guilt, then it is driven by the law. Not grace. We don't give Him our lives because after all, He is God, *although He is.* We don't yield our hearts to Him because after all, He gave His life for us, *although He did*. Ironically, we offer ourselves to Jesus *because* He fulfilled the law on our behalf.

Our heartfelt surrender to Him is more akin to that of a bride to her bridegroom on her wedding night. She tenderly bequeaths herself, *her entire self,* freely, as the proof of her love for him, in response to his love for her. Her desire to give herself away has nothing to do with duty or obligation, but with knowing that she is loved.

We yield our lives to Jesus as evidence of our love for Him, in response to His love for us. We submit our lives to Him when we have seen the Christ—when we recognize our need for a Savior and when we know Him as our Savior, personally. We freely present ourselves to Him when our hearts are captivated by His heart for us. We willingly relinquish the right to ourselves to Him *each time* we look up and seek Him, and find Him, only to discover that He is looking back at us, lavishing us with His intimate love, in all His glory. And we are *changed* by the power of so much love.

Our surrender, and the subsequent offering of our lives, grows into devotion, and devotion drives our worship; our service to Jesus, affectionately; an ongoing decision that we make every single day. One that is *not* rooted in a feeling of love but in a *knowing* of love, our belief that Jesus is the Christ, our Lord and Master, the one who loves us, perfectly.

Belief plays an important role in surrender and therefore in worship. Belief, *faith,* indicates our trust in God for salvation and encourages us toward a sense of commitment and action.

"Believe in the Lord Jesus, and you will be saved" (Acts 16:31a).

And then without works, our faith is dead:

"What good is it, my brothers, if a man claims to have faith but has no deeds? Can such faith save him? Suppose a brother or sister is without clothes and daily food. If one of you says to him, 'Go, I wish you well; keep warm and well fed,' but does nothing about his physical needs, what good is it? In the same way, faith by itself, if it is not accompanied by action, is dead" (James 2:14–19).

As disciples of Jesus Christ, sealed forever with the presence of the Holy Spirit (Ephesians 1:13), our bodies are the offering. Through the prayerful, ongoing, repetitive filling of the *power* of the Holy Spirit (Ephesians 5:18), our service to God becomes our spiritual act of worship—the proof of a life that has been and continues to be transformed to look more like Jesus Christ. Our works do not save us. They are the fruit, the evidence of our belief. After all, even the demons believed that there was one God. Right?

"You believe that there is one God. Good! Even the demons believe that—and shudder" (James 2:19).

Yes, the demons believed, but they were not saved; they did not believe in the atonement, Jesus' finished work on the cross on their behalf. Therefore, they were not surrendered to Him. They did not love Him, serve Him, nor worship Him.

Surrender and our subsequent service and devotion to Jesus are an integral part of worship.

Webster's definition of *surrender* is to give up, acknowledging the power and authority of another, often through the gesture of raising open and empty hands above one's head. When I close my eyes and envision the picture in my mind of a veritable sea of people who love Jesus, raising their open and empty hands above their heads, I see a beautiful picture of surrender—I see worship!

Open Your Hands

When our children were young, we often camped as a family. One of our favorite outdoor activities was to ride off-road motorcycles together through the dirt and the muddy hills of the Shenandoah Mountains. Our son, Joey, drove his first gasoline-powered motorcycle when he was only five years old. I never had the desire to drive a bike of my own. I enjoyed the sport of riding together with the family, but I was always content to ride on the back of my husband's dirt bike.

Until one day when my husband thought it would be a good idea for me to learn.

Our kids were about five and seven years old. We went to a familiar, perfect place to learn to ride the bike: a large, open field that was surrounded by woods. My husband explained the gears to me and showed me how the gas and the brakes worked. And then I was off, riding in circles in the field. Things were pretty uneventful until I got a little too sure of myself. In my relaxed state, I became oblivious to the widening circular path, and before I knew it, I was zipping through the woods like my hair was on fire. It was not a pretty picture. I was completely out of control, screaming as I went, my family in close pursuit, each yelling his or her own set of instructions.

My husband's voice was the loudest. "Let go of the gas! Let go of the gas!" A simple instruction, but no matter; what I heard in my head did not find its way down to my hands. The more out of control I felt, the more tightly I held onto the gas and the faster I went.

Isn't that just the way it is with us? The more fearful we are and the more out of control we feel, the harder we hold on and the more out of control we become. Finally, instead of my husband yelling "Let go of the gas," he yelled, "Open your hands!" A stroke of brilliance. Without even thinking, I opened my hands, loosening the unyielding grip I had on the throttle, and when I did, the motorcycle coasted to a safe stop.

When Mike's instruction was to let go, it seemed like there was something that I needed to do. I was afraid to let go— almost paralyzed with fear. When our response is based in our fear, our instincts will insist that we hold on more tightly every single time. When Mike's instructions changed to "Open your hands," there didn't seem to be the same sense that I needed to do something. When I think about letting go, there is almost an insinuation that there is something I need to do, as opposed to opening my hands, which seems to be less about a work of my hands and more about the position of my heart.

Our son, Joey, on a family camping trip.

Surrender

This is how it is with the Lord. When we open our hands and our whole lives in surrender to Him, we are declaring that our hearts are open and available to His will in our lives—a frightening, yet freeing proposition all at the same time. Who is Jesus, after all, that we should offer our lives to Him? Why should we worship Him? The truth? He is our God, the one who gave His life for us.

He [Jesus] is the image of the invisible God, the firstborn over all creation.

> For by Him all things were created: things in heaven and on earth, visible and invisible, whether thrones or powers or rulers or authorities; all things were created by Him and for Him.
>
> He is before all things, and in Him all things hold together.
>
> And He is the head of the body, the church; He is the beginning and the firstborn from among the dead, so that in everything He might have the supremacy.
>
> For God was pleased to have all His fullness dwell in Him, and through Him to reconcile to Himself all things, whether things on earth or things in heaven, by making peace through His blood, shed on the cross. (Colossians 1:15–20)

So beautiful. We worship Him through the eyes of our faith *because He is our God.*

According to the Bible, worship means to "Ascribe to the Lord, O mighty ones; ascribe the Lord glory and strength. Ascribe to the Lord the glory due His name; worship the Lord in the splendor of His holiness" (Psalm 29:1–2).

We don't "ascribe to the Lord glory and strength" because we have worry-free lives, or because we have more money than we know what to do with, or because we enjoy perfect health or family or children or perfect anything. And we don't ascribe Him glory because of signs and wonders—the mystical occurrences that may or may not be a part of our lives. Of course, the Lord is worthy of praise in all of these things. However, circumstances and situations can and will change from day to day. But God does not … change. He is always worthy of our worship, our praise and thanksgiving. We ascribe glory to Him because He is our Creator and we are His creatures. When we know God personally, we ascribe Him glory for the gospel—the revelation of Himself to us through the person of Jesus Christ. Not the Jesus whom we can so easily invent or imagine Him to be based on our particular need or circumstances at any given time, but the Lord Jesus Christ. The Jesus of the Bible—the one whom we can *know* intimately, but only through spiritual eyes.

CHAPTER 6

Perception—It Matters

My husband's parents have a small cabin deep in the north woods of Wisconsin. As our children were growing up, we vacationed there many times with my in-laws. One year in particular is by far the most memorable. My husband, kids, and I made the long drive to Wisconsin from Virginia in anticipation of a fun family vacation. We were excited to spend time there with Mike's mom and dad, but the drive was very long—especially with two small children. Mike's parents had arrived at the cabin a few days before we did via motor home, so on our first night, my mother-in-law suggested that Mike and I spend the night alone in the cabin and that our kids sleep with them in the motor home. Our kids loved the idea; they jumped up and down at the thought of the adventure, and it appealed to Mike and me as well after such a long drive. A great plan for everyone.

Later on that night, Mike and I drifted into a peaceful sleep that lasted a good few hours, until I was abruptly awakened by a disturbing noise. Since we were nestled so deeply into the dark, secluded woods, my mind immediately began racing to all sorts of imaginative, frightening explanations. Certainly it would not have been unusual for a bear or another sort of wild animal to be outside of the cabin. I lay perfectly still, listening for a few minutes, only to realize that the noise was actually coming from *inside* of the cabin. It was a whizzing, hissing sort of a noise. I shook Mike to wake him, and he listened too—and of course he didn't hear *any* noise whatsoever, never mind whizzing and hissing. After insisting that all was well, he assured me, "There is no noise; go back to sleep." I tried, but I couldn't; I continued to hear the noise; in fact, it was getting louder. Whatever it was it seemed to be right there in the room. With us.

After a few minutes of careful deliberation, I mustered up enough courage to reach my arm out from my protective layer of blankets to turn the light on. I was mortified by what I saw: there, flapping and flailing back and forth across the bed, was an enormous bat. And this bat did not look happy. He was baring his teeth and hissing at us like a rabid cat just inches above where we slept. In record time, Mike and I were now both fully awake and in complete agreement that there was indeed a disturbing noise in the room. We both ran out of the bedroom screaming (at least *I* was screaming) and laughing hysterically. The bat continued to fly around the room for a while before landing on the curtain rod in the room, where he appeared to be resting, hanging upside down and swinging back and forth. We spent the next couple of hours experiencing some of the most excitement we have had in our entire marriage as we attempted to shoo the bat out of the cabin.

We found a broom in the kitchen and used it to chase our intruder, hoping to brush him out the front door. Oddly enough, he had no intention of leaving. We tried swatting him so that we could knock him down and sweep him out. But oh no, this bat was smart. We were no match for him. Each time we swatted him, he would fall to the floor, but when we tried to scoop him up, he would fly up in our faces, and the hysterical laughing and screaming would escalate. We were having so much fun chasing this bat that we were oblivious to how much noise we were making. Without realizing it, we woke up my in-laws, who were now watching us through the large front windows of the cabin, peering in to see what all the commotion was about. Then, when our children woke up to the noise, their grandparents cautiously protected them from the questionable antics of their parents, sending them back to bed.

The infamous "bat cabin".

Now, from their vantage point, all they saw was what looked like my husband chasing me with a broom in the middle of the night—in his underwear. *And I assure you, he was not.* What they didn't see was the bat! They missed the most essential element of this experience, the *reason* for our middle-of-the-night escapade. I learned the next day that my in-laws thought they had inadvertently stumbled upon some sort of a "private moment." Hysterical. Understandably, that was the only inference they could make based on their incomplete, limited information. Their conclusion was based upon their perception.

Perception matters in every area of our lives, particularly in our viewpoint of God. What we believe about God's love for us is one of the most important things about us. It will largely dictate how we live our lives and will absolutely affect our passion for Him. God's love for us is spiritually discerned; it cannot be intellectually discovered. It is revealed by the Holy Spirit through the person of Jesus Christ, the Word of God. It is crucial that we have an accurate perception of God and His love for us. When we know and believe we are loved by God, we are different, affected. When we know we are loved, we love in return.

When my daughter Katie was in the first grade, she bounded home from school one day gushing with excitement as she eagerly exclaimed, "Mom! Guess what? I have a boyfriend!"

I answered, "Really, Katie?"

"Oh yes!" she declared. "His name is Kevin." And she proudly showed me a little necklace that her boyfriend, Kevin, had brought to school for her. Katie told me that she loved Kevin. I asked her why she loved him. Her answer came with a little bit of an attitude: "Mom, because Kevin loves me!"

As women young or old, we need to know we are loved, unconditionally, by God. God created us to know that we are loved by Him. When we believe that God loves us, a response of love is provoked in us for Him. We love Him because He first loved us.

We all learn about love somehow. There have been times in my life when the whole idea of unconditional love has been really hard for me. I learned as a very young child that being loved was directly connected to my behavior. I grew up feeling and absolutely believing that if I was going to be loved, I had to make it happen through my own actions. The Holy Spirit has taught me that God's love is different and that He has already proved

His love for me at the cross, before I even had a chance to earn it or manipulate Him into loving me through my performance. He showed me this through His Word, the Bible.

Questions

I didn't start reading my Bible seriously until I was pregnant with my daughter, but not because I wanted to know Jesus better. That's why I read it now. Back then, I was reading it out of fear and because I was depressed. Consumed with the very real possibility of having yet *another* miscarriage, I was desperate for comfort and assurance beyond myself. I read my Bible looking for comfort, and as I did, I discovered the Comforter Himself. As I read and prayed, the Lord ultimately revealed His love to me in a most unusual way.

At my mother-in-law's suggestion, I started reading the New Testament, beginning in the gospel of John. Ironically, the more I read, the more unsettled I became. Instead of finding comfort, I became disenchanted, even angry. I read about God's love for me and how He had *always* loved me, but I had difficulty reconciling that truth with the experiences I had had as a child. And I had some questions.

Questions like "Lord, if you really love me, then why did You allow so many things to happen to me as a child that were so very wrong? Is it that you really aren't loving, or really not powerful?" It didn't make sense to me. I couldn't resolve what I knew my experience had been with who I was reading God to be. God is love, right? So, if God loved me so much, then why *did* so many difficult things happen to me as a child? Was He just not aware? The answer I was forced into believing was that God *was* aware of what was happening. And beyond that, He was actually present during those times in my life. And He chose to do nothing. What kind of love knows such atrocity and chooses to do nothing? I couldn't see the love.

Along with my questions, I had a bit of an attitude that vacillated between extreme anger and profound sadness. I believed I had a right to some answers, just simple answers—that was all I wanted. Someone owed me an explanation. And I got to be the judge of whether the explanation was sufficient and worthy of my suffering. I mean, I was just a child when so many of these things happened—a small, defenseless child.

At the time, I was seeing a Christian counselor who responded to my questions with a verse from the Bible—Romans 8:28: "And we know that in all things God works for the good of those who love Him, who have been called according to His purpose."

Is it true? Yes. It is absolutely true. But wait a minute. Is our loving Jesus really just about knowing the right answers and being okay with them—just because the answer is biblically correct? Is intimacy even possible in a relationship when one of the two is strong-arming the other into believing something is true? Not likely. I suspect that even at that time in my young walk with the Lord, I believed the verse was true because it was in the Bible. I knew the truth of this verse in my head, but not in my heart; intellectually, but not personally. Intellectual knowledge and personal belief can clearly be two different concepts: the first is what I know; the second has become a part of who I am. However, knowing the truth of this verse did not take away any of what I felt. Instead, it added guilt to my anger, causing me to think I should be able to believe it if it was true.

I tried to walk away from the Lord, but I couldn't—I was constantly drawn back to Him. As much as I wanted to be loved, I viewed my need for love as a weakness. I prayed and asked the

Lord to take this unhealthy emotional requisite away from me. I was just so damaged in my thinking. Once again, I believed someone loved me, and once again, I was wrong. I could not deal with any more rejection. I should have known it was too good to be true. I was mad at myself for believing so easily.

That same week, I heard a sermon taught from the third chapter of Zephaniah. The pastor said that God loves us so much that He actually delights in us. Later that day, I asked the Lord specifically about the truth of Zephaniah 3:17.

"The LORD your God is with you, He is mighty to save. He will take great delight in you, He will quiet you with His love, He will rejoice over you with singing."

As I heard the Lord speak directly to my heart, I wrote His words in my Bible right next to the passage: "All women long for love from their fathers. But what if we didn't have that love? God doesn't fix our lack by removing our need. He satisfies the desire He gave us for love Himself. He sings over us Himself."

Even as I read that today, I am absolutely flabbergasted at the tender goodness of God to give me those words during such a fragile time in my life. God doesn't fix our lack by removing our need! He satisfies our need for love Himself! As I read the Scripture that day, I realized that there was nothing wrong with my desire to be loved. It wasn't a weakness. I was intended to be loved by God all along. But then knowing this just fueled the battle for understanding that was taking place in my mind. If God loved me, then *why?*

I reread the book of John, many times, determined to find the answers to my questions. As I did, I started to *hear* that God loved me. And amazingly enough, I started to believe it—God *did* love me. For a long time, I didn't really understand why I started to believe. It seemed that I somehow began to hear God's voice in my head louder than my own. I still believe that is true. However, recently, the Lord gave me a clearer understanding of how it happened as I once again read the book of John.

I realized that in my honest conversation with the Lord, I was saying to Him, "Look at my hurt. Look at my sadness. Look at my suffering. Look at my wounds." And He said to me, "I hear you. I hurt with you. I am sad with you. I see your wounds. Now, let me show you mine!" I cried and questioned and pleaded and agonized with Him about my wounds, and He showed me His wounds *for me.*

I was wrong in my judgment of God when I wrestled with Him in my thoughts: *What kind of love knows such atrocity and chooses to do nothing?* So wrong. I was, furthermore, wrong in my assessment of God, to think that He did nothing in response to the atrocities done against me—or against us. My way of thinking was flawed. My perception of God and His love for us was skewed; I didn't realize all of the facts. The truth of the matter is that He, Jesus, being in very nature God, did not consider equality with God something to be grasped, but made Himself nothing, taking the very nature of a servant, being made in human likeness. And being found in appearance as a man, He humbled Himself and became obedient to death—even death on a cross! (Philippians 2:6–8).

The truth of the matter is that Jesus Christ, while remaining fully God, humbled Himself, becoming fully man, *human.* He willingly left all the glory of heaven, setting aside the prerogatives of deity that were rightfully His, in order to become a servant for us. He *intentionally* left heaven in order to come to earth; He was born a baby, became a man, suffered, and died the death of a common criminal, although He had no sin of His own. And He did it for us.

That image is so awful and yet so beautiful. God's response to *all* atrocities, *all sin against Him,* was the sacrificial death of His Son for us—for our inherited sinful nature as children of Adam, for our individual sins born out of our sinful nature, and for the sins of others committed against us—all ultimately against God Himself. He died for the sins of the whole world.

Deeply Personal

We were not present when Jesus was nailed to the cross. We did not hold the hammer or pound the nails directly into His flesh. But, it was our sin—the sin of every one of us—that held Him there, in His perfect obedience, as He died a slow, agonizing death with the wrath of God being poured out on Him. It was our sin that kept Him there! The only thing far more tragic than the suffering we experience in this lifetime is the necessity of Jesus' willing, sacrificial death on that cruel Roman cross—for us. All because God loves us. Do you *see* this love? I do. Has God's love become deeply personal to you?

It is the Holy Spirit who reveals God's love for us to us through the gospel. In my own personal journey, He has deepened my understanding of the gospel each time I read the book of John. He taught me about His wounds for me through His Word. It almost breaks my heart when I read these words:

"When they came to Jesus they found that He was already dead, they did not break His legs. Instead, one of the soldiers pierced Jesus' side with a spear, bringing a sudden flow of blood and water. The man who saw it has given testimony, and his testimony is true. He knows that he tells the truth and he testifies so that you also may believe" (John 19:33–35).

The gospel became deeply personal to me as the Holy Spirit caused my heart to believe. The Holy Spirit is the one who causes *any* of us to believe.

"Then He said to Thomas, 'Put your finger here; see my hands. Reach out your hand and put it into my side. Stop doubting and believe.' Thomas said to Him, 'My Lord and my God!' Then Jesus told him, 'Because you have seen me, you have believed; blessed are those who have not seen and yet have believed'" (John 11: 27–29).

Beautiful. Blessed are *we,* who have not seen and yet have believed that "He was pierced for our transgressions, He was crushed for our iniquities; the punishment that brought us peace was upon Him, and by His wounds we are healed" (Isaiah 53:5).

By *His* wounds we are healed.

Please hear what I am saying correctly. I didn't discover intimacy with Jesus *because* of my hurt. My hurt was what drove me to read the Bible, absolutely. However, difficulty doesn't necessarily breed intimacy; loving Jesus passionately doesn't automatically follow difficult circumstances. We are all capable of suffering apart from Jesus and of not going to Him in our brokenness, choosing instead to become angry and resentful. Conversely, we don't have to suffer in order to love Jesus passionately; it is not a requirement for intimacy in our relationship with Him.

Suffering is a normal part of life. We will suffer personally or we will suffer the anguish of watching someone we love suffer. And when we do, *if we turn to Jesus,* the Holy Spirit teaches us about our need to rely on Him for life and breath and all things. He slowly weans us away from our natural "independence from God" and teaches us to be supernaturally dependent on Him.

However, becoming dependent on God is not an end in and of itself in our relationship with Him; *intimacy is.*

We All Have a Story

Our personal interactions with Jesus Christ become our story with Him—His story in us; our testimony of His grace, power, and love in our lives. Our stories are all different. They look different, and they should look different because God is such a personal God. And, however unique, all of our stories with Him are important, every single one of them.

I have counseled many women over a period of many years who have believed that they didn't have a *real* testimony to share about coming to know Jesus personally because their lives prior to knowing Him weren't *that bad.* Such a lie from Satan! Jesus didn't come and die so that we could become "less bad" in our flesh. Apart from knowing Jesus, we aren't varying degrees of *good, bad, or worse* in our sin; we are *dead* in our sin. Jesus suffered and died to give us life, new life in Christ (Romans 6:1–4). Not to make us *better.* Going from being eternally dead to eternally alive in Christ is always a big deal, no matter the circumstances of our life stories that preceded our salvation. The most important part of our testimony with Jesus is when we say, "Then I met Jesus." Let me tell you about Jesus! All of our life stories are important. They are all different, all preparation for what God will ask of each one of us, personally, in this lifetime.

The Holy Spirit reveals the love of God through Jesus Christ to all of us as He deepens our understanding of the gospel, regardless of our prior sin or background, race, religion, or ethnicity. All who believe that Jesus Christ is both Lord and

Savior can experience intimacy with Jesus through the indwelling Spirit, for the glory of God.

The key to loving Jesus deeply is to be absolutely convinced of His love for us. The Holy Spirit convinced *me* of the love of God through the person of Jesus Christ, in my suffering, as I read the gospel of John in the Bible.

I am so glad that my mother-in-law sent me to the Bible instead of trying to answer my questions herself. What a tremendous blessing. The Lord never did answer any of the specific questions I had; instead, He answered the question underneath that I was really asking: "Why didn't you love me?" His answer was simple: "I did love you. I do love you." And I believed Him because of His wounds for me. I do not understand how the Lord replaced my own heart's understanding with the truth of His own, yet I know that He did. And I know that He gave me a love and a hunger for Him that cannot be satisfied. It happened, and continues to happen, as I spend time alone with Him, reading His Word.

CHAPTER 7

Every Day with Jesus

We learn about the *depth* of God's love for us *after* we receive Jesus as our Savior. Apart from the indwelling Holy Spirit, the gospel and the truth of the Bible, the written Word, would not make sense to us at all (1 Corinthians 1:18). It is only through the Spirit that we have the spiritual insight that is necessary to understand what we are reading. When we don't spend time quietly with Jesus, we are not making ourselves available to the teaching of the Holy Spirit through the Word. The loss is entirely ours. We cannot know and be changed by God's love for us through Jesus Christ if we don't know what the Bible says about God's love for us. Apart from knowing the truth of the Bible, we are forced to draw conclusions about God's love for us based on the circumstances of our lives, through our own reasoning, without all of the facts. It is paramount that we, as followers of Jesus Christ, read and know the truth of the Bible.

It is our personal responsibility to learn about God's love for us, who Jesus is, and what it means to be His follower—His disciple. The Holy Spirit is our teacher. He teaches us through our consistent practice of the spiritual disciplines: reading the Bible, studying the Bible, prayer, and meditation—the time we spend quietly, alone with Jesus. As we do our part, the Holy Spirit changes us by causing the truth of what we are reading to become who we are instead of just what we know. We do our part, and the Holy Spirit does His part (John 15:1–8).

Interestingly enough, the need for practicing the spiritual disciplines among Christians seems awkward, misunderstood, or even unnecessary. I think there are many followers of Jesus who want very much to be more like Him but who are unwilling or apathetic in the practice of spiritual disciplines. I believe this is a spiritual battle because this viewpoint is inconsistent with our mainstream ideals regarding higher education.

For instance, it is generally understood that if one wants to become a doctor or an architect or any other sort of professional, one needs to study. We understand that in order to learn, we must be taught. And to be taught, we must participate in the disciplines of education: attend classes, read books, attend lectures, complete internships, and take and pass examinations. We must do whatever is necessary based on the curriculum to complete the degree program. We don't question that these things are our personal responsibility.

The same thing is true in living the Christian life: in order to know Jesus personally and to know what it is to be His disciple, we must individually, intentionally observe the spiritual disciplines. However, there is one major difference.

We learn what it means to be a doctor *before* becoming a doctor. We must learn and then earn the right to be doctors. A college degree is a costly certificate that is awarded *only* when we can pay the price demanded and then prove we are worthy to receive it. Salvation is free. It is a gift given to us by the grace of God, through our faith. Although it is free to us, it is a costly gift. Motivated by His love for us, God Himself incurred the cost, as the price was paid by Jesus Christ. Being worthy is not a requirement. We simply are not worthy. In fact, realizing that we are unworthy sinners is what is necessary. The onus of being worthy, good enough, has never belonged to us. We are the problem; we cannot be any part of the solution. Proving our worthiness to God in order to be a follower of Jesus Christ would evidence Christianity to be a religion that is earned, continually, by our good works. It is not. It is a relationship with Jesus Christ, the one whose righteousness is imputed to us when we simply believe the gospel message personally. We are saved by His perfect work, not by our own. We contribute nothing to our salvation.

However, all that said, it is so important that we also understand that it is not the *reading* of the Word that changes us. It is not the *knowing* of the Word that changes us. The Pharisees read and knew and even memorized the Word more than anyone else. They were religious experts when it came to the Word, and yet they were not changed. The reading and the knowing of the Word did not even cause them to believe, even though they held in their hands the Holy Spirit-inspired Scripture that pointed to the coming of the Christ. They held the knowledge in their hands and in their heads—but not in their hearts. We too can be filled with knowledge, and we too can be religious experts and never enjoy an intimate moment in our relationship with Jesus Christ, the Living Word, absolutely convinced of His love for us.

Study is important. We must read and study the Word in order to know Jesus. We must do our part. Of course. However, we must also walk in concert with the Spirit, experientially, as He—and only He—applies the teaching of the Word, renewing our minds and transforming us more into the image and likeness of Jesus from the inside out (Galatians 5:16; 2 Corinthians

3:17–18, Romans 12:2). Otherwise, the change is only topical and temporary; it *will not* last. It will burn away when we are tested through the difficult circumstances of our lives (John 15:6), or it will melt away when times are easy. The Word will become *what* we know: knowledge. It will not become *who* we are: changed.

And it will not honor Jesus. It will honor us. We will *look* more spiritual, but we will not *be* more spiritual (2 Corinthians 5). We will not be more like Jesus; we will be more like the Pharisees.

When we don't spend time alone with Jesus, the simple truth is that our love for Him will be affected—not His love for us, but our love for Him. We will not know Him intimately. Sadly, the loss will be entirely ours.

Our bodies are the temple of the Holy Spirit—not just the housing or the dwelling place, but the *temple,* the sacred place where the Holy Spirit lives.

As His disciples, remarkably, we can know Jesus experientially, intimately, through His indwelling presence. Intimacy with Jesus is not only possible in the life of the believer; it is what Jesus Himself prayed for us, to God the Father: "Now this is eternal life: that they may know you, the only true God, and Jesus Christ, Whom you have sent" (John 17:3).

The word *know* in this passage is the Greek word *ginosko,* which means "to know" and carries implications of personal covenant knowledge, even marital, one-flesh intimacy. Then in verse twenty of the same chapter, Jesus continues to pray to the Father: "My prayer is not for them alone. I pray also for those who will believe in Me through their message, that all of them may be one, Father, just as you are in me and I am in you" (John 17:20).

Jesus is clearly speaking of a spiritual, intimate knowing, a position and privilege for children of the Living God. Intimacy with Jesus doesn't discount knowledge of the Scriptures. Intimacy occurs when *knowing Jesus* goes beyond our knowledge of the Scriptures. Intimacy with Jesus Christ, *the Living Word* (Hebrews 4:12), knows the truth of the Scriptures personally (Ephesians 3:14–19). We spend time alone with Jesus to know Him, to be more deeply and intimately acquainted with Him (Philippians 3:10) in response to His love for us proven through the gospel. Not for what He *will do* for us. After all, He *has already* given His life for us.

Sweet Revelation

My own personal time alone with Jesus has grown sweeter and more meaningful over time. As I intentionally sought the Lord's presence, the Holy Spirit has lovingly healed my heart and changed my perspective, allowing me to see many of my past life experiences through His eyes. When the Holy Spirit changes our perspective, our need to know *why* and our question, "Where was God?" are replaced with seeing the presence of God in our circumstances. The difficult experiences from my past have not gone away. Nothing can ever change them. Nevertheless, He has graciously allowed me to see them through the lens of the truth that all of life—everything—is for our good and His glory.

As I look back over my life, I can see that I have much to be thankful for. For instance, while I did grow up a victim of physical and sexual abuse, I am not a victim anymore. I am no longer without hope. And because of the abuse in my background, I am passionate about the Lord and excited to tell other victims of abuse—and anyone who will listen—about who God is and the healing power that is found in the person of Jesus Christ. We all need hope. Life can be hard, and I want so much for everyone to know His love, His comfort, His victory, and His grace in their lives. I want so much for God's glory to be seen by all people.

Another thing that I see as I look back is that He completely protected me from a life of prostitution. As a very young teenager, I entered the world of beauty pageants and TV commercials. At that time, I had many opportunities to have harmful, compromising photographs taken and occasions to participate in unhealthy relationships with men. Today, my heart is full of compassion for women who are taken advantage of in similar situations. It's so important to know how much God loves us and how valuable we are to Him. The Lord helped me to see and believe that *all* my guilt and shame no longer exist because Jesus Himself took on the guilt and shame *for all of my sin* through His death on the cross. As a fiercely loved child of the Living God, I will never again be objectified—degraded to the shameful status of a mere object—for any reason. I will never again *be the show*. And there will never be any reason for me to hurt myself again. Not ever. I am so thankful.

The Lord reminded me that as a child, in the midst of abuse, I had many very nurturing teachers who genuinely cared for me, including the teacher who gently, lovingly, and without judgment peeled the dirty scab off my head. And in junior high school, I had a teacher who realized I needed help and talked to me about my depression and assured me that I wasn't "less-than" because I cried at school. He was nice. I have no doubt that he was one of many kind, nurturing men the Lord used in my life to offer me a *healthy* view of men. Isn't that so like God?

The Lord has helped me to remember the many Thanksgivings and Christmases when strangers from area churches brought us food and took time to visit with us. I would watch them and think that one day, when I was older, I wanted to help people too.

When I look back, I see the Lord at a church camp I attended for underprivileged children. I was so homesick the entire week. Every night, my cabin leader would play her guitar and gently sing us to sleep. I don't know for sure, but I believe that the songs she sang were about the Lord because I was so comforted and enjoyed restful sleep, free from nightmares. The Lord was so amazing at this camp; I imagine many people from the church prayed for us underprivileged kids during our stay. Even today, I sleep peacefully every night, free from the nightmares that plagued me as a child. My dreams have become beautiful, often filled with colors that I have not seen anywhere on this earth. God is so good; He redeemed even my dreams.

And the man I was married to before Mike? Forgiveness has taken place between us, both ways. The Lord has graciously restored our relationship together as one of friendship.

The Lord showed me that my mom, even as she dealt with her own struggles, was at times a very touching and hugging kind of mom—and I needed that. My need for physical touch is still very much a part of who I am today.

One of the biggest things the Lord has done for me is allowing me to see my mom as the struggling person she once was and helping me to understand that she was doing the very best she could do at the time. He showed me who she was and how life had been so hard for her. As I came to this realization, it helped me understand why so many things happened the way that they did. Today, my sweet mom is a beautiful Christian woman. She is full of grace, and we have been very good friends for many years. She has given me her blessing to tell my story. I am so thankful that the Lord chose my mom to be *my* mom, and to know that she too is *His*. I am especially grateful that He has granted immeasurable, healing forgiveness in our relationship together.

These changes in my perspective are truly sweet revelations from the Lord.

Please understand, I am not discounting my life that once was by pretending it wasn't that hard, or by convincing myself that things could have been worse. I am not saying that I just needed to have a more positive attitude. No. The little girl whom I once was is still very much a part of the grown woman that I am today; *she is me.* My seeing things differently now comes from believing that God is sovereign and that He is in charge of everything. It comes from knowing that there is a bigger picture here, way bigger than just me, and that the difficult things that happened were just a small part of a wonderful story that God Himself is writing. I am choosing to believe that even my small story is for *His* pleasure, *His* purpose, and *His* glory.

I marvel at the fact that the Lord didn't *have* to reveal any of these things to me, and He was not required to provide the healing that paved the way for the reconciliation that has occurred in my relationship with my mom. He just did, because He is good.

His goodness is especially meaningful in this season of my life because my mom is older now and has many of the health problems that can come with age, including Alzheimer's disease. She is doing pretty well with her Alzheimer's, but as I learn the natural progression of the disease, I realize how much more difficult it would have been if healing in our relationship hadn't begun until now.

What If?

Just this morning, I was talking to the Lord about my relationship with my mom—about the what-ifs. Lord—what if? What if healing hadn't taken place in our relationship? What if my relationship with my mom was still driven by my anger and resentment? What if You had not changed my understanding of who she is and given me an amazing, unusual love in my heart for her? What if You had not torn down the old relationship I had with my mom and created the new relationship we have shared now for many years? Lord, *what if?*

If the Lord's healing forgiveness had not taken place, I would have missed knowing and loving my mom with Jesus. I would have missed being nurtured and loved by my own mother, the way the Lord intended the mother-daughter relationship to be.

However, because of God's grace, I didn't miss anything. In fact, I am astounded by the beauty of our relationship together. It is honest and pure. It is better than good, undefiled by any old hurts or resentments. It is God-centered—a wonderful gift from the Lord. A true picture of the redeeming power and nature of God through the gospel of Jesus Christ. I am incredibly blessed, overwhelmed by His love—almost without words.

I am so glad that today I do not have to deal with any of the what-ifs in my relationship with my mom, that we are so blessed by the Lord. Jesus Himself is the one we share—the one who holds us closely together. He is the one who gave us both the gift of reconciliation that began with forgiveness—His forgiveness of us, individually, and then our forgiveness of each other, which would have been both improbable and impossible left to our own fleshy, prideful desires and lack of power. God is so caring, so amazingly good. In His great sovereignty, He provided all that was necessary so that forgiveness could take place: Jesus Himself, the power of the Holy Spirit, and the willing obedience of our hearts.

Me and my beautiful mom.

CHAPTER 8

Obedience—The Proof of Love

I went to high school in the late 60s and early 70s, a time in our history when rebelling against authority was popular and often more highly valued than obedience. Peace marches and sit-ins typified this cultural phenomenon, and my way of thinking as well. I both marched for peace and sat in defiance.

Even in our culture today, authority is not always valued or even acknowledged. And without the recognition of authority, obedience is never an issue. However, as a follower of Jesus Christ and according to the teaching of the Bible, obedience is a huge issue.

The entire Bible, both Old and New Testaments, is threaded with the theme of obedience, beginning in Genesis. Adam and Eve were both offered an opportunity to obey after God told Adam, "You are free to eat from any tree in the garden; but you must not eat from the tree of the knowledge of good and evil, for when you eat of it you will surely die" (Genesis 2:16–17).

And of course, Adam (and Eve) *did* eat from the tree of the knowledge of good and evil, and the rest is history. We are still affected today by the consequences of Adam and Eve's choice to disregard authority, evidenced by their decision to disobey the Lord, resulting in spiritual *and* physical death.

Then, in the New Testament, Jesus Christ Himself teaches that, as His followers, we show our love for Him through our obedience to Him. Jesus clearly states, "Whoever has my commands and obeys them, he is the one who loves me" (John 14:21).

Our obedience to Jesus is the expression of our passionate love for Him.

Obedience is Jesus' love language; it is how He receives love from us. And it is how we demonstrate our love for Him. It is our passion in action. It encourages our *work* that accompanies our *faith* (James 2:26).

It is our love response to God for what He has already done for us through Jesus Christ: the gospel. Not for the hope of what He will do for us if, after all, we are good, obedient Christians. No. It is our love response to what he has already done for us through Jesus Christ: provided forgiveness of sin, victory over the grave, and the assurance of eternal life through the resurrection.

The gospel is a done deal. It is an historical fact, an actual event, recorded by hundreds of eyewitnesses in a living document—the Bible. Living the Christian life is our love response to the love that God showed us at the cross. We love Him because He first loved us. We love in response to His love. And we prove our love to Him through our obedience to Him—our Savior, our Lord, our Master—as He continually grows and changes our hearts by the power of His grace.

Loving Him

Several years ago, I traveled to eastern Europe on two separate missions trips. The purpose of both was to spend time with kids from an orphanage and to share the love of Jesus Christ with them. As I prepared for the first time away, a good friend of mine counseled me not to go; he thought what I was planning to do was wrong and even heartless—to go and spend time with children from an orphanage, only to turn around and leave them a short time later. I admit I heard what this man was saying, and it caused me to question my decision. From my friend's perspective, it did almost seem like a mean and hurtful thing to do to already hurting children; it didn't make sense to me. However, I believed with all certainty that the Lord was asking me to go, and He had confirmed it through Scripture, so I went.

Both trips included teams of missionaries from both the United States and eastern Europe, and together we worked with the children from the orphanage. The second trip was more difficult than the first.

On our second trip together, we arrived at the camp two days ahead of the children so that we had time to pray together in preparation for their arrival. We waited for them with eager anticipation until finally, the hour came and the busses motored into the camp. As the team swarmed the open field to greet the small travelers, I paused; then I stopped, overcome with emotion, suddenly plagued with memories of my own childhood and the feelings of hopeless despair that were once a nagging, all-too-familiar acquaintance. My insides hurt for the kids. I was sad for them. Sad to know that they probably lived their lives feeling unloved. I hated that for them. It took me a few minutes with the Lord to move beyond the unanticipated, uncomfortable feelings I encountered. Quite unexpectedly, the trip had become very personal. I just wanted to love these kids. I wanted them to know that they were loved. I didn't want them to suffer the way that I had suffered. I *needed* to change their world, to make their lives better somehow.

Before the end of the first week of our time together, I knew I was becoming attached to the kids we were working with. The entire team was. And the kids were becoming attached to us as well. Our hearts were fully engaged; we loved those kids so much.

As this time with the children wound down, I began to think about my friend's counsel. And I started to question the Lord: "Lord, why *did* you send us here?" My confusion was compounded now by my own difficult memories of being a child, and I was almost angry with Him. I envisioned saying goodbye to the kids and leaving them—for the second time. I thought to myself, *Isn't that what their parents did? They left them. They didn't want them, and the kids knew it. And now they'll think we don't want them either.*

As a matter of fact, it wasn't uncommon for parents to leave their kids at the orphanage as infants and then return to pick them up after they turned eleven or twelve years old so that they could use them as beggars or prostitutes to earn money for the family. The European missionaries even told us that they were aware of times when the parents broke the arms or legs of their infants before they brought them to the orphanage so that they would grow deformed. That way, the children would be more effective beggars when they were older. What a difficult image to comprehend, but it truly demonstrates how the children's parents need the Lord too. We all do.

Well, the longer we were there with the kids, the harder it became emotionally, and the more I questioned the Lord. I prayed and asked Him, "Why, Lord? Haven't these kids been *hurt enough?*"

There was one little boy, Joseph, who absolutely stole my heart. He was about eight years old, and he was an extraordinary child: tender, loving, and warm. I first got to know and love Joseph on the trip I took the prior year. Actually, we got to know and love each other. I will never forget one day in particular when Joseph climbed up into my lap and hugged my neck, looking up to me with his big, beautiful, pleading hazel eyes, and told me through an interpreter that "he would be honored to be my son if I would be honored to be his mother."

His words took my breath away, and I just came apart. Through the sobs I was overcome with, and in the grace that the Lord provided, I explained to him that I would be honored to be his mother if it was possible for him to be my son. I told him that I loved him in the same way a mother loves her son and I wished that he could be my son, but it was not possible. My heart was sick. My stomach felt like it was turning inside out. I was sad and hurt for Joseph—and angry with the laws of the government.

At this time in this particular country, the children who lived in orphanages were not legally adoptable. This little boy had experienced nothing but rejection in all of his short eight years. I could tell by his tears that he did not understand. *I* did not understand. And there was no way that I could adequately explain to him what I could not comprehend myself. I didn't know what else I could say to him; what response could I possibly give him? And how could I then say goodbye? Here I was, telling Joseph about Jesus and how wonderful He was and how much He loved him, and then turning around and hurting him by leaving, rejecting him once again. Would he even hear what I was saying? Or would he discount everything he heard because of his pain?

I sat with Joseph for a long time after our exchange of words. We wept together, quietly, as I rocked him back and forth in the same way a mother rocks her child. For that short time, the Lord graciously allowed my mother's heart to love him as a son and Joseph's heart of a child to know the love of a mom. He needed to be loved, and I needed to love him. Also, wonderfully, as I held Joseph, I knew the love of God, almost as if *I* was the child that was being rocked by the mother. It was definitely a time of healing for my own soul as I actively recalled what it felt like to need *and not realize* the touch of my mom when I was a child. I experienced the Lord differently in those tender moments with this young boy, as if through the mind of the child I once was, all while realizing the blessing of being able to offer a mother's touch. All because of Jesus. My own sense of wonder lingered for several days, in awe of the Lord and His very personal gift of love for Joseph and for me. The Lord was so good to orchestrate those precious moments that he and I shared together.

I was so glad when the Lord finally spoke to me during this difficult stage of our trip, relieving me of the heartfelt heaviness and responsibility I felt to fix Joseph's world and reminding me of His love for Joseph. He helped me to see that it is never our job to change anyone's world; that was His work to do. I understood clearly that we were there to share the love of Jesus Christ with the children and the orphanage workers and to tell them about the relationship that they too could have with Jesus. That was all.

The Lord Speaks

The Lord showed me this very truth through my daily reading of the Bible: Matthew 28:19—a very familiar verse, yet how appropriate for that specific day and time. The Lord spoke very clearly to me, as He often does during my time alone with Him as I read the Scriptures.

"Therefore *go* and make disciples of all nations, baptizing them in the name of the Father and of the Son and of the Holy Spirit, and teaching them to obey everything I have commanded you" (Matthew 28:19).

The Lord spoke to me through His Word—and as my Lord, my Authority. I went on this trip because He told me to go. He didn't ask my opinion or my advice. And He didn't ask me to go for my own feel-good gratification. He simply said *go*. And I did go. We did go.

We went, and we loved the children with the love of Jesus Christ, as we were directed to (Matthew 10:42). We supplied them with their basic needs—all of which the Lord provided. And as we did, the Holy Spirit provided us with the platform to tell them about their most essential need: Jesus Christ! The forgiveness of sin that God provides through Jesus Christ is the most essential, basic need of us all.

It is absolutely good and right to lovingly care for the basic needs of others. However—and I can't stress this enough—it is also good and *best* to tell others about Jesus Christ. If they already know Jesus, it is of course best to encourage them in Him. If they do not know Jesus, we should never, ever leave without sharing the hope that is found only through the person of Jesus Christ: forgiveness of sin. Help is good—but *hope* is essential.

And I don't say that flippantly or carelessly. I know personally what it is like to be hungry. I know the suffering and pain that come from not being sufficiently fed or lovingly cared for. I understand having no hope. I am so thankful that now I know Jesus. Now I have hope—hope in the circumstances of this lifetime and the security of salvation in the next. Jesus Christ is our hope.

The life we see on this earth is not all of the life there will be. The Bible says that life on this earth is visible for a little while, and then it disappears. We do not know what will happen tomorrow. Life as we know it is temporary; a vapor, a wisp, a puff of smoke (James 4:14). Therefore, suffering in this lifetime is temporary also, but it doesn't have to even exist in the next.

We will all live beyond this lifetime as we know it, for all of eternity (John 5:28–29). Those who know Jesus will one day rise *to live,* and those who do not know Jesus will one day rise to be eternally condemned. Life is eternal for everyone—whether we have forgiveness of sin through Jesus Christ or not. The determining factor for how we will spend eternity is *forgiveness.*

Those who know Jesus personally will live *with* Him, in the perfect, peaceful presence of God, for all of eternity. Those who do not know Jesus personally will live *apart* from Him eternally—forever subjected to God's wrath, punishment, and consequences for sin. The choice is ours.

We All Have a Platform

We went to eastern Europe with a specific purpose: to minister the love of Jesus Christ to the children in the orphanage. We made sure that that they had food, water, shelter, and medicine even though we couldn't fix their world. But Jesus didn't ask us to. He simply told us to go. And that is what we did. He told us to tell the children about Him. That is what we did. And we went with Jesus, not in place of Him, our act of obedience acknowledging the power and authority of the Lord Jesus Christ.

I was so thankful the Lord spoke to me and gave me His perspective and His peace through the Word. It was so personally kind and loving of Him, exactly what I needed from Him at that very moment. The morning came for the children to return to the orphanage, and as the goodbyes began, the air was filled with sobbing and wailing—both from the children and from the missionaries. It was almost unbearable. The children had to be physically pried off of us and almost forced onto the bus. They didn't want to go, and we didn't want to let them go. I was pleading with the Lord to help Joseph, and all of the children and me, to give us His strength. I heard His voice over and over in my head: *I have them; it is okay. Let them go.* Even so, when the time came for me to say goodbye to Joseph, he and I had to be wrenched away from one another. I believed that the Lord had him and all of the children; I did. However, I loved this beautiful child like he was my own. He had captured my heart; I didn't *want* to let him go. As the children left the camp that morning, all we could hear were their sobs and screaming through the closed windows of the bus they were traveling in. After the rumbling of the bus could no longer be heard, the sounds in the air were those of soft sniffles and quiet prayers from the missionaries as our raw emotions settled into the Lord's peace.

During the time I spent with the children, the Lord lovingly gifted me with His perspective and His peace regarding my own childhood. He showed me that when I was a child, *He had me too,* in the same way that He had the children from the orphanage. And somehow, that day, that revelation from the Lord was sweet, even life changing. It remains life changing today. Revelation follows obedience; life-changing moments of personal healing occur most as we walk with the Lord in service to Him.

I was thankful to the Lord for the opportunity to tell the children and their adult caregivers about Jesus' love for them and how they could have their own personal relationship with Him too. The Lord knew that they would need His peace in their suffering too. He is so good. And I was earnestly thanking and praising Jesus for loving and caring for all of the children, although, to be completely honest, I was praying and praising Him especially for little Joseph. I don't know if the circumstances of Joseph's life improved or even changed after we left or not. But I do know that I will see him again because while we were there with him, he was one of the many children who heard the truth of the gospel and trusted Jesus Christ as his Lord and Savior. Praise God! I am so thankful that the Lord sent us, and I am so thankful that we went. I am thrilled to know that one day I will see Joseph again—in heaven, the beautiful young boy who still holds my heart today.

The Lord provides each one of us time and opportunity to share His love with those who don't know him personally. The whole world is our mission field. Our spheres of influence will, no doubt, be unique to each one of us according to our circumstances or seasons of life. We may have opportunities to tell others about Jesus as we visit with other moms at play groups, or with our fellow employees, or with those who are fearfully anticipating a doctor's report, or with older folks who reside in nursing homes, or with people we have never met at the grocery store, or with sweet children a thousand miles away in a foreign land. In Christ, we are the living letters, the living proof of God's love, evidenced through our love of others. Wherever we are, that is our platform.

CHAPTER 9

Obedience before Power

When the Lord speaks to us through the Bible, no one should cause us to question what we hear from Him. When my friend told me his thoughts—that it was wrong for me to go and spend time with the children from the orphanage—I should have turned to the Scriptures to see if what he said was true, since God will never ask anything of us that contradicts His own truth. If I had, I would have found that James 1:27 commands us to look after widows and orphans in their distress. Clearly, if I had searched the Word first, it would have been an easier trip for me.

Then again, I would have missed the rich time of conversation the Lord and I had while I was in eastern Europe and the personal, intimate time He took to speak to me through His Word. As He spoke to me, I knew without a doubt that the Lord Himself had sent me on this trip to love and care for the children and to share the greatest gift ever with them—Him!

Something I have really learned about the Lord from reading the Bible and experiencing life with Him is that He will engage in conversation with me about anything. Anything. He will lovingly listen to any thought or question I might have. But I also know that eventually He will remind me that He and only

He is God, that His ways are not my ways and that His motives are *always* pure and *always* good. He is sovereign over all things.

Jesus Christ is both our Lord and Savior. He is our Lord—our Master, our Authority. And He is our Savior—the acceptable sacrifice who paid our sin debt. Jesus has never been our Savior apart from our Lord (Luke 2:11, Acts 2:36). And we don't make Him our Lord; He isn't waiting to be assigned the position of Lord in our lives. It is a matter of acknowledgment, not assignment. All authority in heaven and on earth has been given to Jesus (Matthew 28:18). As His followers, our obedience to Him is the proof of our love for Him, and our acknowledgment that He is our Lord. And sometimes, He is pretty creative in how He lets us know what He is asking of us.

A Father's Nudge

My husband and I love everything about the ocean, especially boating. Several years ago, we were cruising together on Chesapeake Bay. It was a picture-perfect day; the bright blue sky was a breathtaking backdrop to the enormous, fluffy, white fair-weather clouds. But I wasn't enjoying the beautiful day; in fact, I hardly even noticed it because I was so miserable. While my husband was down in the cabin, I was on the upper deck, having been assigned the job of watching for crab-pots and other things floating in the water. But I wasn't doing a very good job of it; instead, I sat with my dog and talked—or more like cried out—to the Lord. I was a frightened, agonized mess. I knew the Lord was calling me to a speaking ministry. He had spoken to me through the Bible, and He had presented an opportunity to serve Him in this way—I had committed to speak at a women's retreat. But I was petrified. I really did want to do what I believed the Lord was asking. My spirit was completely willing, but my flesh was pitifully weak. And my flesh was winning. I was nearly paralyzed with fear.

After a time of debating with the Lord—then consulting my own flesh—I decided I was not going to do it. I wasn't going to speak at the retreat. But what would I tell the nice lady who had asked me? I sat on the top deck of our boat and tried to come up with a convincing, feasible way to back out of this commitment while saving face and not appearing too "unspiritual." To put it bluntly, I was trying to think of the cleverest lie that would sufficiently release me from my promise without letting down the kind woman who had invited me to speak.

I was in deep, sad self-pity when all of a sudden I heard a flapping, scratching noise and felt the air moving behind me. I stood and turned, only to see the biggest bird I had ever laid eyes on perched on the railing just a couple of feet away from where I was sitting. This creature was a good three feet tall from its feet to the top of his head. It was gigantic—and I was trapped. I was literally trapped between this giant—and man-eating, I was certain—creature and the inside wall of our boat. There were only about three feet between us, and there was no place for me to go. And there it just sat—staring at me.

I instinctively thought of my dog. She was sitting on the seat directly beneath the railing where the bird-monster was perched. Her nose was actually resting on the railing just a couple of inches from its giant, fierce-looking talons. She didn't budge. I loved my dog, and I rehearsed over and over in my mind exactly how I would rescue her if and when this giant man- or dog-eater decided to pick her up and carry her away. But the creature didn't even acknowledge her; it just stared at me. It was creepy, and I was horrified.

Being careful not to make any startling, sudden movements, I cautiously called down to Mike, my strong, capable husband, the captain of our vessel. Surely he would rescue me. It seemed like forever before he answered and came up to see what was going on. When he did, he stopped just short of coming up the steps to where I was, telling me to hold still. *No problem,* I thought. And then he said to me—and I quote—"I am not coming up there."

Now, in my husband's defense, he is a very brave man. He is a rough-and-tumble, hockey-playing, hunting and fishing kind of a guy. He is also a very wise man, and I trusted him.

For the time being, I was okay with Mike not joining me on the upper deck because I had more time to think—and I had a plan. I suggested to him that he get the boat hook, a long pole that we use to grab dock lines when we dock the boat. He ran back down into the main cabin to grab it. He was gone for what seemed to be an eternity, leaving me and our dog defenseless and alone with this domineering mass of wings and talons.

Mike finally returned to the deck just short of where we were: the dog, the bird, and I. He extended the pole and held it in front of the bird, and to my surprise, it tried to step out onto it. Have you ever been to a parrot show and watched a trainer hold a pole in front of a parrot, and then watched as the parrot stepped onto the pole as the audience erupted in applause? Apparently, winged creatures do that instinctively, because this one did, and it was wild and untrained. However, the bird was too heavy, and the pole kept falling under its weight. Extremely frightened now, I erupted into tears.

I honestly thought, *Okay, Michael, you have a pole, and there is a giant bird standing way too close to me, staring me down. I am probably going to die, so just hit the bird.* However, Mike is also a nature-loving kind of guy, and I knew he wasn't going to hit *anything* unless he had to. The pole just wasn't working. And the more hopeless it looked, the harder I cried.

Mike started yelling and dancing, trying to scare the imposing creature away; it didn't scare easily. Actually, it didn't scare at all. Strangely, no matter how much noise my husband made or how much he jumped around trying to scare the bird away, it never once turned its head to look at him. It only stared at me. Strange.

Remarkably, even though I was so afraid, I couldn't help but notice how truly magnificent this creature was. Its head bobbed up and down and twitched in a peculiar fashion. It was wet, and its feathers were stuck flat against its chest. I could actually see its muscles flexing as it inhaled and exhaled. It was the scariest, yet most beautiful and majestic, creature I had ever seen in my life. We just stared at each other, this massive bird and I.

My husband tried the pole thing again, and this time, he was successful in causing our uninvited guest to lose balance. As this happened, it fell backward a bit and then flew away. We watched in awe as this tremendous creature sailed on the wind, farther and farther away from us. It was massive, even bigger than I had realized. Its wingspan must have been six or seven feet.

Mike hurried me below into the cabin, thinking the bird might have been sick because of its unusual behavior. He also thought that it might come back. It didn't, though, and I was glad.

The first thing we did early that evening after we arrived back home was a search on our computer: *birds on Chesapeake Bay*. Mike and I recognized our visitor at the same time—we were both sure of it. Imagine our surprise to see that the creature that had caused us so much fear and panic was a *bald eagle!* We hadn't realized this at the time because its head hadn't developed its white, tufted feathers yet. This indicated that it was a young eagle, less than five years old.

So, a bald eagle had landed on our boat for no apparent reason and stared at me for ten long minutes. How can that be? Eagles just don't swoop down on people's boats and challenge them to staring contests. It just doesn't happen. Because it was so unusual, I thought it had to be the Lord. I didn't know why or how, but I believed it sure could have been the Lord. There was no rational explanation for this unusual encounter.

I Believe

So I asked the Lord about it. I searched the Scriptures. I found several different verses that talked about eagles. However, I still didn't have any understanding of what the Lord might have been saying. Maybe it was just happenstance, but if the Lord was speaking to me, I didn't want to miss it. I asked my husband, my mom, and Iva, my mentor of many years, what they thought. They all encouraged me to keep praying and asking the Lord to reveal what He was showing me. And pray I did.

Soon after, a friend of mine gave me a book to read about different types of birds. In reading it, I discovered a very interesting fact about the habits of eagles. When baby eaglets are mature enough to leave the nest but are reluctant to fly away, the father eagle will put the food for the baby on the limb of a nearby tree instead of feeding them the usual way, mouth to mouth. The hope is that the young bird will get hungry enough and risk flying to the tree in order to reach the food.

However, sometimes it doesn't work because the eaglet will choose to go hungry instead of making that perilous first flight.

He is just too afraid. In this case, the father eagle (much to the mother's dismay, I am sure) will gently push the baby out of the nest. However, when he does, he doesn't just watch the baby tumble down and hope for the best. He swoops down above, but very close to, the baby, and the aerodynamics of his flight give the eaglet *lift*. As the eaglet gets caught in the updraft of its father's wings, it flies. The father uses the power generated by his own wings to enable the baby eaglet to fly. Isn't that a beautiful picture? So much love and power and encouragement. As soon as I read this, I knew what the Lord was saying to me.

When the eagle landed on the boat, I was in the middle of an agonizing conversation with the Lord, telling Him I was too afraid to speak at the women's retreat—or anywhere else, for that matter. I knew that through the encounter with the eagle on the boat, along with my time of study and prayer that followed, the Lord was saying to me, "Jaye, you know me. You know that I love you. Do you trust me enough to let me push you out of the nest? And do you have enough faith to know that I will lift you up with wings like eagles, and that I won't let you tumble down alone, hoping for the best? Do you believe me?"

And I said, "Yes, Lord. I believe."

It was only after I really prayed and asked the Lord about the experience on the boat that I realized what He was saying to me. I am sure that if I had not prayed and asked the Lord, my unusual encounter with the eagle would have been exactly that, an unusual encounter, instead of, ultimately, a treasured time of hearing from the Lord—however He chose to speak to me. He cares so much for us. He isn't just a mean taskmaster. He cares about our fears. He loves us passionately, and He empowers us to do what He asks of us. I am forever amazed by Him.

Three months later, I spoke at my first women's retreat. And the Lord did, in fact, do what He promised me He would do. He lifted me up "with wings like eagles" (Isaiah 40:31). He didn't let me fall. He enabled me to do what He asked of me. He gave me His strength. He caused me to run without growing weary. He enabled me to walk, and not to faint. He spoke *in* me and *through* me, way beyond my natural abilities. He was teaching me to trust Him. All for His own glory.

Love Isn't Enough

Love can be a powerful motivator. But when we are serving the Lord for His Glory, our love for Him simply isn't enough. We need the Lord's power, *the Holy Spirit,* to do what He asks of us. Consider Peter, a disciple of Jesus Christ. Peter loved Jesus passionately, so when Jesus told Peter that he would deny Him three times the night of His arrest, Peter responded to Jesus declaring, "Lord, I am ready to go to with you to prison and to death" (Luke 22:32–33).

In Matthew's account of the same story Peter boldly promised, "Even if I have to die with you, I will never disown you" (Matthew 26:35).

And Peter meant what he said. We have no reason to believe that Peter's statement of love was anything but honest and heartfelt. His response to Jesus was the expression of his love for Jesus.

However, as we read Peter's story further through Luke's account, we find that Peter wasn't able to do what he promised, no matter how powerfully he loved Jesus. His love alone wasn't enough.

Jesus is arrested: "Then seizing Him, they led Him away and took Him into the house of the high priest. Peter followed Jesus at a distance. But when they kindled a fire in the middle of the courtyard and had sat down together, Peter sat down with them" (Luke 22:54–55).

Peter followed Jesus—but at a distance. Then he sat down with those who accused him, identifying himself with them instead of with Jesus, proven through his actions.

"A servant girl saw him seated there in the firelight. She looked closely at him and said, 'This man was with Him.' But he denied it. 'Woman, I don't know Him,' he said" (Luke 22:56–57).

Peter answered, denying that he even knew Jesus.

"A little later someone else saw him and said, '"You also are one of them.' 'Man, I am not!' Peter replied" (Luke 22:58)

In his response, Peter denied that he was a follower of Jesus.

"About an hour later another asserted, 'Certainly this fellow was with Him, for he is a Galilean.' Peter replied, 'Man, I don't know what you are talking about!' (Luke 22:59–60a).

This time, Peter denied that he was even from Galilee, therefore denying any possible association with Jesus whatsoever—and proving that Jesus was right. Peter did deny Jesus, three times.

Next is what I believe to be the most painful *and* the most beautiful part of the text.

"Just as he [Peter] was speaking, the rooster crowed. The Lord turned and looked straight at Peter. Then Peter remembered the word the Lord had spoken to him: 'Before the rooster crows today, you will disown me three times.' And he went outside and wept bitterly" (Luke 22:60b, 62).

Notice how Jesus intentionally turned and looked directly into Peter's eyes *as* Peter denied Him. The word *looked* here is from the ancient Greek word *liefeld,* which suggests a look of deep love, concern, or compassion. It was Jesus' look, His expression of *love*, that caused Peter to remember what Jesus had told him earlier that day—that he would deny Him three times. Jesus was right in His prediction, but He didn't look at Peter with disappointment or disgust. And He didn't turn away from Peter, but toward him, out of love for him, realizing Peter's sorrow *with* him. Peter was instantly convicted of his sin, not only that he denied Jesus, but also the sin of pride that caused him to believe that in his own power he could never deny Him. Peter wept bitterly as he experienced godly sorrow, the gift of sorrow God gives us that leads to repentance and that leaves no regrets (2 Corinthians 7:10).

Peter had walked closely with Jesus for more than three years by that time. He knew Jesus well, and he loved Him. Peter was promising to follow Jesus always, even to death, but in His own power—purely out of his love for Him. But his love wasn't enough. And the Holy Spirit hadn't been given yet, so Peter lacked the power to do what his heart desired.

Later, though, after the coming of the Spirit (Acts 2) and the birth of the church, we see Peter again, preaching to the men of Israel. He preached the gospel; the death, burial, and resurrection of Jesus Christ, with power beyond himself—the power of the Holy Spirit.

"This man [Jesus of Nazareth] was handed over to you by God's set purpose and foreknowledge; and you, with the help of wicked men, put Him to death by nailing Him to the cross. But God raised Him from the dead, freeing Him from the agony of death because it was impossible for death to keep its hold on Him" (Acts 2:23–24).

"Therefore let all Israel be assured of this: God made this Jesus, whom you crucified, both Lord and Christ" (Acts 2:36).

The men of Israel were convicted by the Holy Spirit:

"When the people heard this, they were cut to the heart and said to Peter and the other apostles, 'Brothers, what shall we do?'" (Acts 2:37).

Don't you love the question, "What should we do?" It is a wonderful question to hear in response to our sharing the gospel with someone!

"Peter replied, 'Repent and be baptized, every one of you, in the name of Jesus Christ for the forgiveness of your sins. And you will receive the gift of the Holy Spirit'" (Acts 2:38).

Baptism is evidence of their salvation, as opposed to a work toward their salvation. Then the text tells us:

"Those who accepted his message were baptized, and about three thousand were added to their number that day" (Acts 2:41).

Three thousand! Peter preached the truth of the gospel—in love with Jesus and empowered by the Holy Spirit. A commanding, God-glorifying combination, both for Peter and for us.

Jesus did predict that Peter would deny Him three times, but He also promised that He would pray for Peter, and that his (Peter's) faith would not fail, and when Peter turned back, he would strengthen his brothers. Jesus was faithful, even when Peter was not. And of course, Jesus was right. In Acts, chapter 2, we see Peter's faith strong, strengthening his brothers, but this time with a power beyond his own. The power of the Holy Spirit!

Faithful

The coffee shop in Venice was charming—elegant, actually—but its adjoining powder room was not. As I excused myself from the table and began to walk down the hallway to the ladies' room, I sensed danger. However, I needed to use the restroom, so I continued on. The powder room door was just ahead on the left side of the dimly lit hallway; I could see it already. I could also see a small group of suspicious-looking men. They saw me too—and headed straight toward me.

I quickly stepped into the powder room and locked the door behind me. Soon after, the men began to pound on the door, screaming obscenities and demanding that I come out. I remained quiet and gave them no answer, which provoked them to rattle the metal handle on the door. It broke in their aggressive attempts to get in; they were so angry.

I started to scream, really scream, for my daughter and my friends who were enjoying their cappuccinos in the safety of the coffee shop—but to no avail. They didn't hear me. Through tears, I prayed, "Jesus, help me! Jesus, help me!" After a few more long minutes, the pounding stopped, and all appeared quiet. The men seemed to have gone, but how would I know for sure? And I couldn't leave even if I wanted to because now the doorknob was broken. I was at a loss as to what I should do. I was so far down the dimly lit hallway that no one could hear my screams for help. My fear had me backed up to the wall as far as I could go. I was violently shaking—waiting—unsure of what to do. *If only I had listened to the still, small voice in my head that had warned me: danger.* But I didn't.

After a few minutes of waiting and praying, I tried the handle again. Maybe I could fix it somehow and get it to work. To my surprise, it worked perfectly; the door opened without any problem, and the hallway was empty. The men were gone—and I was safe.

The still, small voice I heard warning me of danger was the Holy Spirit. Yet, even in my disobedience, the Lord protected me.

The doorknob worked perfectly when I entered the room. And it locked perfectly, with no problem. However, when the men tried to enter the room, the Lord blocked them by causing the handle to spin; I saw it spinning myself. There is no explanation other than the Lord's divine protection, protection that I would not have known or experienced apart from the Holy Spirit's prompting and encouragement to *turn the knob* on the door and then to return unharmed to my daughter and my friends in the coffee shop. Praise God!

Sometimes I think we just need to *turn the knob*, so to speak—to step out in faith even if we have been disobedient. We will most likely have the consequences of our disobedience; I was terrorized in a poorly lit hallway as a result of choosing not to obey. Nonetheless, I experienced the power of the Holy Spirit, and moreover, even in my lack of faith, the Lord remained faithful.

Coffee shop friends! My friend Kay, and me.

Me, my daughter Katie, and Kay's daughter, Katie.

CHAPTER 10

The Holy Spirit

In the Olympic Games of ancient Greece, the marathon was the quintessential event, featuring only the most spectacular athletes. This demanding contest of endurance remains popular today with many of the rules and regulations intact, with one important distinction. The athlete running in a marathon today runs alone, *solo*. In the ancient Greek games, the contender had the advantage of inviting someone to run the last few miles of the race with him—someone who would be waiting at a pre-designated place along the route. This person would be ready to run, full of energy; not having spent himself on the many miles already completed, he would be indispensable to the tired athlete. His role wasn't to take the place of the athlete, but to run with him, *alongside him to help;* to encourage him, to remind him that he was well-trained and prepared for the event, to exhort him when his feet were bleeding and his legs felt like they wouldn't carry him one more stride. His job was to lead, guide, and direct the runner and to help him resist the temptation of taking the easier route—straying from the determined path. His work was to remind him that he was not alone, to enable him to finish the race, and to remind him of the reason he was running: to finish well, victoriously, for the prize that awaited him at the finish line. The teammate to the runner was called the *parakletos—one who is called alongside to help.*

Just before Jesus died on the cross, He lovingly spoke this amazing passage of Scripture to the disciples:

"I will ask the Father, and He will give you another Counselor to be with you forever—the Spirit of truth. The world cannot accept Him, because it neither sees Him nor knows Him. But you know Him, for He lives with you and will be in you. I will not leave you as orphans; I will come to you" (John 14:15b-18).

Through these intimate, comforting words of Scripture, when Jesus referred to "another Counselor," He chose to use the Greek word *paraklete.* He spoke of another Counselor: the Holy Spirit. He is saying that the Holy Spirit—the One just like Himself, who at that time lived *with* the disciples (Jesus)—would soon come to live *within* the disciples (the Holy Spirit).

And the Holy Spirit did come to live within all believers. Fifty days after God resurrected Jesus from the grave, the disciples witnessed the birth of the New Testament church at the Pentecost, through the coming of the indwelling Holy Spirit. It wasn't until after the Spirit came with power (Acts 1:8) that Jesus gave the Great Commission to the disciples and to us, to "Go and make disciples of all nations, baptizing them in the name of the Father and of the Son and of the Holy Spirit" (Matthew 28:19).

We are the hands and the feet, and the Holy Spirit is the power.

The Holy Spirit is *God.* He is God, the Holy Spirit: the indwelling person and presence of Jesus Christ in the life of the believer (Galatians 2:20). He is the third person of the Trinity. God the Father, God the Son, and God the Holy Spirit are all equally one God, sharing all the attributes of God. Although they are three distinctive persons, they are collectively one God. There is only God.

Our first encounter we have with the Holy Spirit is when we become Christians. He is the one who invites us into a relationship with God through Jesus Christ. The Holy Spirit convicts us of sin, of righteousness, and of judgment and then shows us the truth of the gospel at the time of our salvation. He continually reveals the truth about who we are in light of a holy God and causes us to realize the ways in which we fall short of God's glory as we live the everyday, transforming life of a Christian.

Apart from the power of the Holy Spirit, we cannot know God or His powerful love for us. He is the one who causes the gospel message to make sense to us, and He is the one who appropriates the power of God in our lives.

The Holy Spirit is also the Comforter—the Helper. He comforts us through the truth of the Word, which doesn't necessarily equate to a *feeling* of comfort. How, for instance, can we enjoy a feeling of comfort if we are being convicted and therefore burdened with the sin of unforgiveness? The truth of the Word, the Bible, does not change, and the Holy Spirit will never provide consolation that is void of truth.

The Holy Spirit reveals, leads, guides, directs, and empowers us to do all Jesus asks of us. And He always exalts Jesus, bringing Him glory through the circumstances of our lives, every day— no matter how far along we are in our walk with Jesus.

Believe and See!

I don't think I started to really mature in my faith until I had been a Christian for about four years. Sure, I loved Jesus, and I knew that one day I would die and go to heaven, but there wasn't much evidence in my life that I was His follower. Despite my lack of spiritual maturity, I was still blessed to experience the power of the Holy Spirit in my life in very specific ways.

Mike and I had been married for three years when our first child, Joseph Michael, was born. My pregnancy with Joey was plagued with problems from day one, and complete rest proved to be the solution to all of them. After nine full months to the day, we had a beautiful son. We were elated.

Joey with his beautiful wife, Nicole.

When Joey was about a year old, Mike started to travel quite a bit with the company he worked for. He was typically gone for three to four days a week and then home for the long weekend—just long enough for me to get his laundry washed and repacked. It was during this time that I became pregnant again and had another miscarriage—my fourth. And then, a few months later, I became pregnant again, with my daughter. This time, I was proactively relegated to full-time bed rest. With my history of miscarriages, there was no need to take any chances. However, this time of "taking it easy" proved to be a bit more challenging with a one-year-old son. Thankfully, Joey was an incredibly easygoing little guy. He was quite happy to spend time with my mother-in-law and Mike's sisters, and they were more than happy to take him whenever they could. Joey loved being with them, and they were wonderful with him.

Apart from being very apprehensive, the first two months or so of the pregnancy with my daughter were fine; with no problems at all, this pregnancy seemed to be different. So, with the doctor's approval, we took a family vacation, a restful vacation, nothing too strenuous or physically demanding. We visited my brother and his family in Vermont.

Between Mike and my brother and his family, Joey was completely doted over and well taken care of. And I was able to comfortably rest, following the doctor's orders precisely. But no matter; toward the end of our visit, I was terrified to discover that I was beginning to experience complications with the pregnancy. I was all too familiar with the signs of having a miscarriage, already having lost four babies. I was plagued with anxiety, so afraid of losing this baby too. I just wouldn't be okay with it. I remember thinking, *I just cannot deal with losing another baby*. I wasn't a mature Christian, but I was a desperate Christian. I slipped into the bathroom at my brother's house and dropped to my knees in prayer. And I sobbed. Just sobbed. And I prayed, "Lord, no!" I begged the Lord to help me somehow. I cried out to Him, "Lord! I can't do this again. Not again, Lord. Please don't ask this of me; it has happened too many times." I remember in my frustration pleading with Him, "Please hear my prayer, Lord. Please." I remained in the bathroom for about fifteen minutes, just crying out to God. Loudly. Desperately.

I regained my composure the best I could and once again joined my family, still fearful. Later on that evening, my brother asked if we would like to participate in their family's celebration of the Advent calendar. I didn't know what an Advent calendar was. My brother explained that for each day of Advent, the children would open a window on the calendar and there would be a piece of candy, along with a message for that day.

We watched as the kids got their candy, and then my brother took the message and read it out loud. It said, "Be anxious for nothing, but in everything, by prayer and supplication, with thanksgiving, let your requests be made known to God." I couldn't believe what I was hearing. I was sitting next to my husband on the couch, and impulsively, I squeezed his knee and blurted out, "God just spoke to me."

I didn't know a lot about the Bible, but I knew those words were from the Bible. And I knew that God had spoken directly to me. I instantly made the connection between crying out to God in the bathroom and these words from the Bible. This time, I cried out to the Lord again, a cry of "Thank you!"

I was amazed that He had listened to me and that He had heard me. As I look back on that day, I realize that the situation didn't change—the complications continued throughout the duration of the pregnancy without any assurance from the Lord that everything would be all right. He simply told me not to be anxious. He cared about me. He didn't fix the situation, but He heard me *and* He spoke to me. I was utterly fascinated by His power. From that moment on, I was quick to share my heart with Him because He listened—He heard—He answered.

Restless and Unsettled

In the fifth month of my pregnancy, my unborn daughter became very impatient, and I went into pre-term labor. My doctors explained the risks to us—and they were frightening. And as the risk increased, my need for God increased. I just prayed and prayed, and although my prayers weren't eloquent or fancy, I pleaded with God for my baby to be healthy.

Our life at home had become a bit of a routine: I would stay in bed all day—at least, as much as I could with a one-and-a-half-year-old son. Then, when the contractions started, I would call my husband home from work. And then we would go to the hospital, where I would receive an increase in medication to stop the contractions. And then we'd go home. A couple of months into this routine, we made our usual trip to the hospital, but we soon discovered this visit would be very different from the others.

As soon as we arrived at the hospital, I began to feel very restless and unsettled. For some reason, *everything* in me believed that my daughter needed to be born. Right away. I immediately told my doctor, and of course he disagreed. He explained that at only seven months along, it was just too early—that there was too much risk in terms of her overall development. And I certainly understood the risk—in fact, just a week earlier, a good friend of mine had delivered her baby two months early, and he was born with serious neurological complications. So I understood intellectually, but there was something inside of me that just couldn't let it rest. I knew that my daughter needed to be born. *Immediately!* My doctor took his time assuring me that he would know when to deliver her and that I just needed to trust him. He was trying his best to calm me down, but it wasn't working. In my eyes, the situation was escalating in urgency; I was feeling anything but calm as I pleaded with him to *please* just deliver my baby girl. I felt like I was losing my mind. My husband didn't know what to think. *I* didn't know what to think.

Amazingly, my doctor relented and proceeded to deliver our precious daughter, Katie, by Caesarean section. As I was being wheeled to the operating room, my doctor said to me, "Now, Jaye, I don't know if she is going to be okay or not." I insisted that she would be fine—not even understanding myself why I was so confident. He just shook his head a bit, as if to think that this poor woman just didn't get it. And I *didn't* get it; I didn't understand at all. However, I did know that my baby girl needed to be born. And what a little chunk she was. At the time of her birth, she weighed six pounds and four ounces and was actually a little chubby at only seventeen inches long. The doctors were just as surprised as we were; they had anticipated her birth weight to be somewhere between two and three pounds. After her delivery, she was rushed off to the neonatal intensive care unit before I was given a chance to see her.

The morning after she was born, my doctor came to see me. He quietly came into my room and sat at the edge of my bed. He was crying as he spoke. "You know what? I don't really understand what happened yesterday. I don't usually deliver babies because the mom thinks it would be a good idea, but if I had not delivered her just when I did, she would have died." He went on to tell me that Katie had a problem with her heart—a condition that causes the heart to periodically stop beating. *She had a problem with her heart that we couldn't see until she was born.*

I completely believe that the urgency I felt that my daughter needed to be born came from the Holy Spirit. And I believe that the doctor delivered her because of the Holy Spirit. It was the power of God! I was a new Christian, not mature in my faith at all, and God revealed Himself to me, just as He does to *all* Christians through the Holy Spirit. The Spirit of God is not limited to—or by—our spiritual maturity. He reveals His power to us through the eyes of our faith as we pray to our heavenly Father. We believe, and therefore we see!

He Hears; He Cares

Along with her heart condition, Katie was also born with sleep apnea, which meant she could and did stop breathing anytime she slept. Our doctor told us how fortunate we were that she was born at that particular hospital because they happened to have the best neonatal intensive care unit in the area. He said any other hospital might not have even tested her for the typical premature birth problems because of her high birth weight. At the time, my husband and I agreed—how lucky. Today, as we have both matured in our relationships with the Lord, we clearly know that it was not luck—it was God. There is no need for luck when we have the power of almighty God in our lives.

I did not see Katie until she was three days old. Every minute that I was apart from her was agonizing. It felt like my own heart was being ripped from my chest. I desperately needed to hold my baby but couldn't because I was sick—quarantined away from everyone, including Katie, with a case of Roseola. Katie was also quarantined in the NICU as a precaution, just in case she had been infected with the virus through me. The very first time I ever saw her was from a distance, through the window of the NICU. I was shocked to see all the wires and machines she was attached to. As I watched through the window, an alarm sounded, and Katie was suddenly surrounded by a large team of doctors and nurses who immediately began to resuscitate her. I charged into the NICU past the nurses' station, terrified by what was happening. I watched as they began to attach her little body to a ventilator, but then I was quickly escorted—or more like *pushed*—out with the promise that someone would be with me shortly to explain what was going on. I remember thinking, *What? No. This is not okay. I am not okay.* I cried all the way back to my room, feeling so alone and afraid, desperately seeking God. Once again, I heard His voice clearly in my mind: "Be anxious for nothing; be anxious for nothing." Honestly, though, the almost unbearable feelings of anxiety did not magically evaporate; however, those anxious feelings were beginning to mingle with a sense of wonder—fascination, actually. I was awestruck by the fact that once again, I prayed and once again, the Lord spoke. I know that He did. I heard His voice in my mind, undoubtedly. He was showing me His power.

I wasn't a spiritual giant or a biblical superstar; I was just me, a baby Christian. I gladly praised the Lord and thanked Him for hearing my voice and for His very personal, cherished response. Moreover, somehow in the midst of the anguish that I felt through and through, I *became* less anxious, almost unconsciously. He gave me His peace. I began to experience His peace. I was so honored that He would speak to me—that He would care enough to teach me. He is a deeply personal, loving, caring, powerful God.

We brought Katie home from the hospital along with a monitor that, when attached to her with wires, would monitor her heartbeat and pulse while she slept. An alarm would sound any time there was an interruption of her breathing or heartbeat.

A few times each night, we would awaken to the sound of the alarm, sending us running to her room to pinch and poke her until she caught her breath. Most times, I was on my own when it came to monitoring Katie, since my husband's job once again required him to travel three to four days a week.

It was a difficult time for me, personally. I was so empty of myself. I suffered from sleep deprivation, postpartum depression, depression in general, and the heaviness of the responsibility I felt for both of my children, with and without special needs. I remember looking down at them and thinking that I would do anything for them. I would give either one of them my own breath if I could; I would have given them my life.

Interestingly enough, it was just three or four months prior to this point in time that I began to struggle in my relationship with the Lord, questioning His love for me. Ironic, isn't it? I understood as a mom, absolutely, that I would have given my life for my children because of my love for them, and all the while, Jesus was showing me that He, in fact, had given His life for me because of His love for me. *The Lord sure works in mysterious ways.* He is so wonderful.

Our doctors told us to expect Katie to wear her monitor for a full year, but when she was nine months old, my mother-in-law and a group of ladies from her church came to our home to pray for Katie to be healed. They anointed Katie's head with oil and prayed that she would be healed—and she was. From that day forward, she never had another episode with her breathing or heartbeat while she slept. *Ever!* The Lord in His great power healed our baby girl.

That day at my brother's house, when I slipped into the bathroom and dropped to my knees in prayer, pleading with the Lord for His help, I had no idea how the story would end.

When the Lord spoke to me, He didn't tell me how it would end. He simply told me to *be anxious for nothing,* and that He would provide me with His peace. As He spoke those words to me, He, however, knew how the story would progress. He knew that He would let me know when Katie needed to be born; He knew Katie would be a bit chunky; He knew Katie would have issues with her heart and her breathing. He knew I would desperately need Him again when I saw Katie being resuscitated. He knew He would provide all that was necessary for her care, and He even knew He would heal her of these very specific problems. He knew all along. I did not. All He asked of me was to trust Him, rest in Him, be anxious for nothing, and He would supply the peace I needed. And I did. And He did. The Lord also knew that as I walked with Him during this time, He would *begin to* teach me to trust Him, to depend on Him, to lean on Him, and to love Him passionately. He is a God of His Word. *He is a God of His Word.* Our God can be trusted, if only we will look to Him and listen through the Word.

None of us know how our stories will end with Him. Right? Oh, but wait a minute—yes, we do. As children of the Lord Jesus Christ, all of our stories will all end the same: face to face with Jesus. Absent from the body and present with the Lord, without any cessation of life, in the presence of Jesus Himself (2 Corinthians 5:8). Until that day, the Bible is full of promises and precepts about how to live *this* life, all of the days, the easy days and the more difficult, intimately with Him.

This story that is so much a part of my life is now Katie's story with the Lord too. Katie loves Jesus, *passionately.* Every day as she walks with Him, He continues to honor and glorify Himself in and through her life. He is so good and so powerful.

Katie loving Jesus in Africa.

We All Have a Purpose

God created every one of us on purpose, with purpose: to live our lives with Him passionately as we serve Him every single day. Jesus Christ is both our example of passion and our reason for passion.

As I read through the Gospels, I can't help but be awestruck by the phenomenal singular focus, unwavering devotion, and powerful love that Jesus Christ demonstrated as He lovingly obeyed the perfect will of God the Father: to die on the cross for mankind. He knew the love of the Father.

My challenge to you is this: read the Gospels, all in one sitting if possible, whether it would be your first time or your one hundredth time. Why? Because, it matters; our understanding of the gospel *matters*. If we have little knowledge of who Jesus is and the significance of His perfect life, death, burial, and resurrection, there is a good chance that we will live defeated lives, lives that *even for believers* don't reflect the glory of God. Our personal relationship with Him comes with power and authority: the power of the Holy Spirit and the authority of the Lord Jesus Christ.

It is the same power of the same gospel that saves us and then empowers us to grow and to be changed. It is the same power that allows us to hope and be healed, to live our lives passionately for Jesus, in His beautiful grace, even when life is hard. And it's the same power that even returns us to God if we have walked away from Him. No matter the reason.

CHAPTER 11

Stars in My Eyes

It was midnight. The new moon was almost invisible, evidenced by its lack of reflection against the black water of Biscayne Bay. The hour was late, and the sky was dark. My husband and I were sailing between Fort Lauderdale and Elliot Key, Florida, on our twenty-five-foot-long sailboat. We were newly married, and this was our first overnight trip together on our boat. We were more than excited.

When the wind died off, characteristic of the sunset, we pulled the sails down and opted for motor power. After several hours of clipping along at a steady pace, we stopped abruptly when the long keel of the boat (the long part that hangs down directly beneath a sailboat) firmly planted on the ocean floor. We were aground. Mike skillfully attempted to maneuver the boat off the bottom, but to no avail. We were sufficiently stuck in the muck, smack-dab in what we thought was the center of the channel—the charted, designated roadway for boaters, if you will. Somehow, we had wandered slightly off course.

Without the benefit of sunlight, or even moonlight, we could not be easily seen by a passing vessel; therefore, we were in danger of being hit by another boat. We were in the way, and we needed to move.

My husband quickly determined that our problem was simply a matter of physics. The problem was that the keel of the boat had dug straight down into the mucky ocean floor. The solution was to tip the boat, and consequently the attached keel, to one side, liberating it from the stubborn bottom. Once it was free from the unrelenting grip, we would be able to motor freely through the water, once again underway.

The plan? One of us needed to do the "tipping up," and the other needed to skillfully drive the boat off the bottom.

Since Mike was the skillful driver, my job was to shimmy out to the end of the boom that was now extended out to the side, perpendicular to the boat, and then hang there. The hope was that my weight would be enough to tip the bottom of the boat up sufficiently, allowing him to simultaneously drive the boat into deeper water. And that is exactly what he did.

When Mike asked me to crawl out to the end of the boom and hang there for fifteen minutes, I didn't even think about the school of hammerhead sharks we had seen earlier that evening. As I swung from the boom with the movement of the water, my feet dangling just inches above the slapping waves, I didn't consider what might have been lurking just beneath the surface of the dark water. I didn't think about the danger of the situation at all. Instead, I was excited to be part of the team, happy to help. I was unafraid, blinded by the stars in my eyes, certain that my new, wonderful, heroic husband would never ask anything of me that was dangerous. I trusted Mike completely. First love is reckless; it abandons itself to the object of its affection. First love simply loves, as opposed to loves *because*; it is covenantal, not contractual.

Mike and I ready to set sail!

Jesus, Our First Love

There is a passage of Scripture about first love. The apostle John tells of an encounter he had in a vision from Jesus Christ while in the Spirit (Revelation 1:9). This is not the revelation of John himself, but of Jesus Christ, penned by John. Jesus is speaking to the church at Ephesus—and He is speaking to us.

"I know your deeds, your hard work and your perseverance. I know that you cannot tolerate wicked men, that you have tested those who claim to be apostles but are not, and have found them false. You have persevered and have endured hardships for my name, and have not grown weary. Yet I hold this against you: You have forsaken your first love" (Revelation 2:3–4).

In this simple yet insightful text, Jesus is affirming the church at Ephesus; this church was a solid church. They worked hard and persevered, their doctrine was pure, and they had tirelessly endured hardships for the name of Jesus Christ. Nevertheless, Jesus held something against them. Something serious, remarkable: they had forsaken their first love, literally. They had turned away from, *left,* their first love.

This is an amazing passage of Scripture to me because it really shows Jesus' heart for us. He cares about our love for Him. The church at Ephesus had grown in their knowledge *of* Jesus Christ, but not in love *with* Jesus Christ. The love relationship they had once experienced with Jesus, individually and collectively as a church, had become a relationship of doctrine without love. They were spiritually good-looking, religious, and hard-working, but had no love in their hearts for Him. Jesus held this against them, and He holds it against us. The interweaving of doctrine and love characterizes the Christian life (1Timothy 1:3–5). Doctrine apart from love can be cold and methodical, while love apart from doctrine can be sentimental and sloppy, discounting the cross of Calvary.

What is it in the life of the believer that causes us to turn our backs on Jesus, our first love? What is it that happens to us that reduces our love relationship with Jesus to a religion of doctrine, a set of rules apart from love, intentionally turning our hearts away from Him?

I think there are a few answers to this particular question, but the one the Lord brought first and foremost to my mind has to do with losing heart.

We turn our backs on our first love when we believe that our first love has turned His back on us; when we begin to measure God's love for us through the circumstances of our lives instead of the gospel. We lose heart when we believe He has withdrawn His heart from us.

Don't Lose Heart

One of Satan's greatest ploys is to entice us away from the truth of God's love for us through Jesus Christ, with the single hope of causing us to lose heart. It is so easy for us to lose heart, isn't it? We lose heart when the discouragements of everyday life coerce our focus away from God, consequently robbing us of our spiritual vision and causing us to look inward instead of upward. I understand losing heart. I have suffered agonizing torment in my whole person as I have falsely measured God's love for me through what could be seen naturally in my flesh as opposed that which could only be supernaturally discerned in my spirit, by faith. The Lord has taught me—and continues to teach me— that His love for us must be measured by the cross, where it was proven, not by the circumstances of our lives, good or bad. It is essential for us as Christians to be convinced of God's love for us through Jesus Christ, through the cross; it is our lifeblood.

Because our relationships with Jesus can only be compelled by *His* love for us, it cannot be driven by *our* love for Him. Our love for Him, however genuine, can change, be overpowered, or be tempered by the hardships and adversity we endure. Our passionate love for Him can excite us, inspire us, or even motivate us to serve Him when life is easy; but it is simply not enough when our pain and suffering lead us to lose heart, falsely believing that He has turned His back on us.

Where Are You, Lord?

This wasn't exactly one of the brightest ideas I have ever had. My mom, who has Alzheimer's disease, and I, who struggle with learning disabilities, were attempting to assemble a piece of furniture together, a small nightstand. *What was I thinking?* Actually, I think I *wasn't* thinking. It was a disaster. There was a time in my mom's life when she was actually very competent at this type of work, very capable of precisely following instructions. She used to love to assemble model planes consisting of hundreds of small, intricate pieces. However, the Alzheimer's has robbed her of the ability to consistently reason sequentially, compromising her ability to follow step-by-step directions. Me? I was never good at following written directions, step by step or otherwise.

After an hour or so, we realized that it just wasn't going to happen. There was no way the vast collection of tiny pieces that now covered my mom's living room floor was going to become a nightstand. The furniture was going back into the box and back to the store. We were both frustrated. I found it almost comical that we had attempted such a project, considering our limited collective reasoning skills, but my mom did not. She was cognizant of the fact that this was something she could have done at one time, but no longer, and in her frustration, she became angry. In her irritated state, she began to speak to me in a way that was reminiscent of how she used to talk to me before she knew Jesus and before He healed our relationship together. Her critical, demeaning words cut me like a knife.

At first, I just kept thinking, *I know it is the Alzheimer's speaking, Lord; I know it is.* But I quickly reached a point where I couldn't continue to listen. It truly was the Alzheimer's, but it was too hurtful, too familiar. I was surprised by how quickly my heart was affected, and my emotions regressed back to those of the small child I once was. I was also taken aback by how easy it seemed for me to be tempted toward unbelief, to forget God's love and His power that were evident in the restored relationship that I now share with my sweet mom—*to lose heart.* Raw with emotion and plagued with fear, I became angry. Not angry at my mom, but angry that those feelings could still try to affect me the way they once did, as though the Lord had no part in the matter. I felt weak: spiritually, physically, and emotionally. I knew that I needed the Lord.

So I went for a walk—a very long, fast-paced walk with my earphones pressed tightly into my ears, listening to my worship music turned up as loud as I could bear. I immediately chose the song I knew I needed to hear. As I listened to the lyrics "My eyes have seen the glory of the Lord!" I was desperately explaining to the Lord that no, I was not willing to give up the mom I knew and loved to the mom I used to know. *No, Lord, I am not willing. Nor do I believe that I have to, because "My eyes have seen the glory of the Lord."* I told the Lord that even if my mom's behavior changed toward me because of the disease, I was unwilling to accept the fact that I would be affected in the same way I was as a child. No; it would not happen, because *my eyes have now seen the glory of the Lord.* The longer I prayed, the faster I walked. And the faster I walked, the more earnestly I prayed. I asked the Lord to send someone to encourage me. I needed to be encouraged, tremendously. I was a crying, hurting mess. I asked and therefore believed with all my heart that He would send someone.

My walk dead-ended in a small picnic area along the shoreline of a riverbank. I perched myself up on the top of a picnic table, my feet planted on the bench, and I waited expectantly. I was certain the Lord would send someone; after all, I had asked Him to, but beyond that, I knew that He knew I needed to hear from Him. I pulled my earphones out of my ears as I waited so that whoever He sent could freely speak without concern of interruption. I attempted to make eye contact with everyone who passed: moms pushing strollers, men who worked at the paper mill nearby, couples walking along the waterway, people walking dogs, anyone and everyone. I prayed for everyone who passed, that they would have the courage to speak and the ability to know that I was the one they were supposed to speak to. I waited and waited and waited, but no one stopped. No one made eye contact with me. No one spoke to me, not one single person, not even a hello.

I was thinking, *Where are you, Lord?* It was starting to get late, and I felt the need to get back to my mom's apartment, even though I had not heard from the Lord yet. But at least, I thought, I could listen to my special worship music during the long trek back. With earphones decisively placed, I once again pressed play on my iPod, anticipating the beautiful music. But no! I had inadvertently turned the dial on the device, and without my glasses, I couldn't see it well enough to find the misplaced song. Once again, the tears began to flow. This time, it was more of a pity party; first the Lord didn't encourage me, and now I couldn't even listen to my worship song.

In my frustration, I said, *Lord?* Then, in anger, I pushed play anyway. This is what I heard: "Grace and peace to you from God our Father and the Lord Jesus Christ."

My misplaced song had been divinely replaced with a verse from the book of Ephesians; the Holy Spirit was speaking to me through the Bible I have loaded on my iPod. The Lord was encouraging me *Himself.* Read these beautiful, intimate words: *Grace and peace to you [Jaye] from God our Father and the Lord Jesus Christ.* Okay, then. Grace and peace it is! I heard it. I accepted it and believed it. In His very personal exhortation, the Lord reminded me that my mom and I both belong to Him. He lovingly brought to mind that He, the Lord God almighty, is on the throne, sovereign over all things, and that my mom is in His more-than-capable hands. He assured me that He will continue to be a part of our beautiful, restored, God-centered relationship together, regardless of the outward, temporary, non-eternal circumstances of our lives. Only God can cause me to think the way that I did. Praise Him! Now that I am once again convinced of and enthralled with His love for me, my eyes will continue to choose to see the glory of the Lord. I will not lose hope. *We* must not lose hope. We have Hope, eternal.

"God so loved the world that He gave his only son, that whoever believes in Him shall not perish but have eternal life!" (John 3:16).

And, "Therefore, we do not lose heart. Though outwardly we are wasting away, yet inwardly we are being renewed day by day. For our light and momentary troubles are achieving for us an eternal glory that far outweighs them all. So we fix our eyes not on what is seen, but on what is unseen. For what is seen is temporary, but what is unseen is eternal" (2 Corinthians 4:16–18)

Praise God!

CHAPTER 12

Remember, Repent, and Return

Has It Happened to You?

What if we have lost hope? What if we have become jaded by the circumstances of our lives and actually use our feelings as a barometer to measure God's love for us? What if we are no longer convinced of God's love that He proved at the cross? What if we don't have love in our hearts for Him, even as we attend church every single week? What if, tired and worn out, we are going through the motions of what it means to be a spiritually good-looking Christian? Or what if we know Jesus personally but have not been inside of a Bible-believing church for months, or even years? What if we have lost heart, walked away, turned our backs on God, and forsaken Him?

The Good News of Jesus Christ remains the Good News! The Lord, in His goodness and grace, made a way back for us. The solution to these questions is found in the Bible, once again in the book of Revelation: "Remember the height from which you have fallen! Repent and do the things you did at first" (Revelation 2:5a).

The solution to turning our backs on our first love is to remember, repent, and return, individually and collectively as a church.

Remember

"Remember Jesus Christ, raised from the dead, descended from David. This is my gospel" (2 Timothy 2:8).

In this passage, Paul is exhorting Timothy to remember the gospel accurately, that Jesus was fully man, *a descendant of David,* yet fully God, *proven through the resurrection*—the great proof of the legitimacy of the Messiah, Jesus, the Christ, the only acceptable sacrifice for our sin. We are exhorted to remember who Jesus is, what He did for us, and why He did it.

When we don't spend time reading the Word, the magnificence of the gospel can fade into nothingness. Our relationship with Jesus Christ can become one of religion instead of one of grace. Consequently, we can go through the motions, do church really well, but all without the thrill of our first love for Him. When we are no longer amazed by God's love for us we can lose sight of His forgiveness and His complete acceptance of us. Without intentionality on our part, the gospel message can just become ordinary vernacular in the church instead of the most amazing truth that we will ever know. When we don't spend time alone with Jesus, we can lose heart and become overwhelmed by the cares of the world instead of captivated by perfect love. We must go back to the basics: reading the gospel and asking the Holy Spirit to deepen our understanding of God's love for us. We must be convinced of His love for us in order to be compelled by it so that we don't lose heart in the difficulties of life. I love that the relationship we have with Jesus is the only relationship we will ever be a part of where the love was proven for us before the relationship began.

"But God demonstrates His own love for us in this: While we were still sinners, Christ died for us" (Romans 5:8).

Repent

Repent from what? Turning our hearts away from Jesus—forsaking our first love. Is it a sin *not* to love the Lord our God with *all our hearts* and with all our souls and with all our strength? Yes, it is.

"Love the Lord your God with all you heart and with all your soul and with all your strength" (Deuteronomy 6:5).

"Love the Lord your God with all your heart and with all your soul and with all your mind and with all your strength" (Mark 12:30).

And, is it a sin if we don't love our neighbor as ourselves? Yes, it is.

"The second is this; Love your neighbor as yourself. There is no commandment greater than these" (Mark 12:31).

I am personally so thankful for the gift of repentance. I do love Jesus—but not like I should. Honestly speaking, I don't do anything like I should. None of us do. We don't and we won't live the Christian life perfectly this side of heaven. Therefore, repentance is a beautiful thing.

Repentance is our response to godly sorrow, which results from a heartfelt conviction that is given only by the Holy Spirit when we have offended God with our sin (2 Corinthians 7:10); hence, it is a gift from God (John 16:8). Repentance is essential to salvation, and it remains essential in the ongoing life of the believer because *sin* is ongoing in the life of every believer.

Repentance is:

- a change of heart (Matthew 21:29)
- followed by a change of mind (Mark 1:15)
- characterized by a change of behavior (Matthew 3:8)

As followers of Jesus, we repent in response to the Holy Spirit's revelation and conviction of our sin. In our obedience to Him, the Holy Spirit changes our hearts and then empowers and enables us to turn around and to walk away from our sin, our hearts once again turned toward God. We don't have the ability to change ourselves. The Holy Spirit is the change maker. Our part is to respond with obedience to the conviction of the Spirit through the surrender of our will to His.

Sin and Repentance

I flew into the grocery store thinking it would be a quick in-and-out, but apparently so did many other shoppers. It was late on the evening before Thanksgiving, and the store was jam-packed with dozens of patrons making last-minute purchases. The checkout lines were already as long as the store was deep. I paused for a moment, considering the necessity of my forgotten items, and quickly concluded that they were a must. Oh well. I collected the ingredients that I needed and found my way to the end of the quickly lengthening line.

As I got closer to the cash register, I was pleased to see that the cashier was my grocery-store friend; the woman whose line I frequented routinely for my weekly grocery store purchases.

I noticed that she looked tired. When it was finally my turn, I set my items on the counter as I asked her, "How are you?" Her response was honest. She said, "Not too good." Her eyes seemed to be pleading with me for understanding. She explained that she was tired and that her body ached from standing on her feet for so many hours. She continued to say that she was lonely and that the holidays were hard for her. I was surprised that she shared as much as she did, so personally, considering the length of the line and the audible, escalating sounds of disapproval that were coming from those who waited their turn behind mine. I am sure that they had hoped their last-minute trip to the store would be a quick in-and-out too.

The Lord was prompting me to encourage her, to tell her about Him. I knew that He was. However, I was petitioning Him to consider the time and date; it was late, the day before a major holiday. Lord, I thought, this clearly cannot be the best time to talk to my friend. Not when there are so many anxious, tired, and probably hungry customers in line, evidenced by the critical chatter that grew louder and stronger with every word that my friend and I exchanged. Their message was clear: *pay the bill and move on.*

No problem, Lord, I reasoned in my mind. I *will* talk to my friend, but *not* today; I will talk to her on Friday, the day after Thanksgiving. Friday made more sense. The store would be less busy; we would have more time to talk. One or two days won't make any difference at all, I told the Lord as I also convinced myself. After all, I really needed to consider those who waited in the long line behind me. I left the store assuring my sweet acquaintance that *I would be praying for her.* She smiled, faintly, and thanked me.

As I drove home, I confidently told the Lord that I was willing to be obedient, but on Friday. Friday would be better. I was sure that He understood. Although, as hard as I tried to convince myself that *Friday would be better*, I had already begun to recognize the Holy Spirit's conviction; a nagging sense of being unsettled that I could feel down deep in my spirit: *I didn't do what the Lord had asked of me.*

Bright and early on Friday morning, I returned to the store in search of my friend, only to realize that she was not at her register. I searched the store for her, but when I did not find her, I asked another employee if she was scheduled to work that day. His body language seemed awkward considering the simple nature of the question. He summoned the manager, who inquired as to my relationship with the woman. "Friends," I said.

"Oh, I am sorry," he said. "She died. On Thanksgiving Day."

What? "No, no!" I argued, "You don't understand. Not *my* friend! I just saw her on Wednesday evening. She was fine."

He walked with me to the bulletin board at the front of the store and removed a poster with her picture on it, and he asked, "Is this your friend?"

"Well, yes," I said, "But you don't understand. She was fine when I saw her on Wednesday evening." The poster included information about a memorial service that was to be held at the local community center. I could not believe my eyes, or my ears. I started to cry. He expressed his sorrow a few times, asking if we were very good friends. I could not respond. Overwrought by emotion, I ran from the store to my car, where I doubled over, racked with sobs. What had I done? Or, more to the point, what had I *not done?*

All I could say was, "Lord, I am sorry. I am so, so sorry. Please forgive me, Lord. I am so sorry." I was distraught. Once at home, I instantly went to my office, where I spent a long time with the Lord, my face to the floor, sorry for my arrogance, sorry that I had reasoned my plan to be better than His. I was sorry that I had not shared the gospel with this woman when the Lord asked me to. For a brief time, I felt the weight of her salvation as my responsibility, but I was thankful when the Holy Spirit reminded me that *my* obedience had nothing to do with my friend's salvation. Salvation is the LORD's business, and thankfully, there is nothing that we can do to thwart His plans in terms of salvation—or anything else, for that matter.

I was most sorry for the fact that the woman, *my friend,* did not know God's love for her, through me, as she and I stood face to face during the final hours of her life on this earth. It broke my heart to know that she was so alone. Through my delayed obedience (which is really just a pleasant way of saying disobedience; sin), my actions proved that I was ultimately more concerned with pleasing those who were waiting in the line rather than loving the Lord through my obedience to Him, sharing His love with my grocery store acquaintance (Luke 10:29). This was the heart of the matter, the gut-wrenching point of godly sorrow that led to my repentance.

Again, I am thankful for repentance, the amazing gift that releases us from the feeling of guilt that can fester in our hearts and render us ineffective in the kingdom of God. Because repentance affects the quality of our relationship with God. Sin creates a barrier in our fellowship with Him, but through the beautiful gift of repentance, the Holy Spirit restores our broken fellowship; we return to Him.

David's Prayer

Listen to the heartfelt words that David prayed to God after his sin with Bathsheba:

"Against you [God] and you only have I sinned and done what is evil in your sight. Create in me a pure heart, O God, and renew a steadfast spirit within me. Restore to me the joy of your salvation and grant me a willing spirit to sustain me." (Psalm 51:4, 10, 12).

I love that David used the word *restore* (in terms of the joy of the Lord's salvation), the implication proving that David *already knew* God. To restore is to *bring back*. He repented *as a believer* in God.

Repentance releases us to (once again) joyfully love God with our hearts, souls, minds, and strengths and to (once again) return to Him, lovingly serving Him with our lives. David continued to pray: "Then I will teach transgressors your ways, and sinners will turn back to you. Save me from bloodguilt, O God, the God who saves me, and my tongue will sing of your righteousness. O Lord, open my lips, and my mouth will declare your praise" (Psalm 51:13–15).

David sought God in his sin—maybe even especially in his sin. Convinced that he would be released by God from the agonizing guilt that he experienced as a result of his sin against God, David's prayer crescendoed beyond acknowledging his sin and even beyond thankfulness, culminating in his stated intention to joyfully serve God once again.

Return

Return to Jesus, the one who has loved us all along, the one who died for us. Once we become Christians, we can never lose our salvation (John 10:28–29), even if we turn our hearts away from Him. Our invitation to pray, *to come before the throne of grace,* is an eternal invitation. We always, *always* have the right to come into the presence of God. Even beyond that amazing truth, the Lord Himself always wants us to come into His presence. He woos us over and over again in the Word to come to Him.

"Come to me, all who are weary and burdened, and I will give you rest" (Matthew 11:28).

"You will see me and find me when you seek me with all your heart" (Jeremiah 29:13).

"Ask and it will be given to you; seek and you will find. Knock and the door will be opened to you" (Matthew 7:7).

Remember! Repent! Return! Come back. It is not too late, no matter why we have turned or faded away, intentionally or unintentionally. Jesus already knows whatever it is that is keeping us from Him. Is it our pride that causes us to withhold our hearts from Him? Does our pride contribute to our losing heart? Or are we perhaps stuck in sin and afraid to be honest with our brothers and sisters in Christ?

Have you ever shared honestly about sin in your life with a fellow believer and been judged or criticized instead of loved compassionately and encouraged with the truth? I have. It is unacceptable, especially in the church. We simply must have the freedom within the body of believers to speak openly and honestly, to be authentic. We must be able to share our sin struggles candidly without fear of being chastised or marginalized by fellow believers. It is imperative among Christians that we be able to stand up and say, "I have a problem"; to confess our sins to one another and pray for each other so that we may be healed. "The prayer of a righteous man is powerful and effective" (James 5:16).

It is vital to the life of the church that we be free to be honest. Never for the purpose of being coddled in our sin or to have others justify our sin, but to be *prayed for,* encouraged, exhorted, and directed back to the love, forgiveness, and acceptance of Jesus Christ. Honest sharing leads to healing as opposed to losing heart, *when* the sharing is heard in love, with grace. It doesn't matter if we have lost heart because of the circumstances of our lives or due to our past or present sin; the genuineness of our lives must be paramount over our invented, protected personas because all of us will die a physical death one day. We will pass from this life to the next, and then it will frankly not matter how spiritually good-looking we are today, this side of heaven. It will instantaneously be unimportant how many people we have impressed with our spirituality or wowed with our giving, or how many Bible verses we have memorized, or how pretty our prayers are.

The one thing that will matter, however, is having a personal relationship with God through Jesus Christ.

Jesus Himself said, speaking to Nicodemus the Pharisee: "I tell you the truth, no one can see the kingdom of God unless he is born again."

And then Jesus told Nicodemus: "I tell you the truth, no one can enter the kingdom of God unless he is born of water and the Spirit" (John 3:5).

Born of water—Jesus Christ, the Living Water—and born of the Spirit—the Holy Spirit!

The only possible way to have a personal relationship with God is through Jesus Christ: "I [Jesus] am the way and the truth and the life. No one comes to the Father except through me" (John 14:6).

CHAPTER 13

Love, Prayer, Beauty, and Light

---- ❦ ----

Loving Again

P aul teaches us that we can once again be convinced of God's love for us through Jesus Christ as we pray through the power of the Holy Spirit.

In a beautiful passage of Scripture (Ephesians 3:14–19) Paul prays for the Ephesian church, a body of believers who already knew Jesus personally. As he prays for them, he teaches us how to pray so that we can grasp in our hearts the powerful love Jesus Christ has for us. Paul approaches God reverently, kneeling before Him. He asks that God, out of His glorious riches, may strengthen the Ephesians with power through His Spirit, *the Holy Spirit,* in their inner being—their hearts—so that Christ may dwell in their hearts permanently, by faith. He prays that they, being rooted and established in love, *in their knowledge of God,* may have power together with all the saints, to grasp how wide and long and high and deep is the love of Christ, and "to know this love that surpasses knowledge" (Ephesians 3:19a).

He is praying that they know Jesus personally, intimately—not apart from their intellectual knowledge of Him, but beyond it. Fascinating. Our relationships with Jesus are intended to be experienced, alive, and intimate—nothing less than passionate.

If we believe we have left our first love, we must remember, repent, and return to Him. Not for salvation, as we cannot lose our salvation, but for relationship. If our relationship with Jesus has become one of doctrine with no love in our hearts for Him, we must once again discover His love for us, intimately, beyond our knowledge of Him. As Paul demonstrates through this passage of Scripture (Ephesians 3:14–19), the only way back is by prayer and through the power of the Spirit. So we pray.

Prayer

As children of the living God, we are invited to approach the throne of grace with confidence for help in our times of need.

"Approach the throne of grace with confidence, so that we may receive mercy and find grace to help us in our time of need" (Hebrews 4:16).

The word for *confidence* in this verse is the Greek word *parrhesia,* meaning *freedom of speech.* As we pray, we can speak freely to the Lord Jesus Christ, talk to Him honestly about all things. He is our Creator, life giver, and life sustainer. He knows us intimately. He knows our shortcomings, our weaknesses; He knows our hearts, our hopes, and our fears. Therefore, we can talk to Him truthfully and openly. Our prayers don't need to be filled with impressive religious words in order to be heard. When we pray, we are just sharing our hearts and listening to His heart for us. The Lord hears our prayers, no matter the level of maturity in our faith. And He answers them according to His will.

Earlier in the same chapter of Hebrews, we are told *why* we approach the throne of grace with confidence: "Since we have a great high priest who has gone through the heavens, Jesus the Son of God," and "For we do not have a high priest who is unable to sympathize with our weaknesses, but we have one who has been tempted in every way, just as we are, yet without sin" (Hebrews 4:14–15).

We pray to our High Priest, Jesus, the Son of God, who *is* God. We pray to Him because He understands. He has suffered all of what we have suffered—and more. We pray to Him for more than just our felt needs. We pray to Him because He is almighty and all-powerful. We pray to Him in worship of Him and to offer Him our thanksgiving and praise. That is why we pray to Him and Him alone. We pray to Him because He is God. We pray to Him *because we can.*

As believers in the Lord Jesus Christ, the miraculous privilege of prayer is ours. Always. Satan would love for us to believe that if we aren't quite sure how to form our prayers with eloquent words from the Bible, then we have no business praying to God. He would also love for us to believe that if we have ongoing sin in our lives, we have no right to go to the Lord in prayer. How often do we think, *Boy, I have messed up so badly I don't feel like I have the right to go to God?* That is such a lie from Satan. As believers in Jesus Christ, it has never been our own goodness that has afforded us His presence; it has always and only been because of *His* goodness that we are invited. It is because of our standing in Christ that we have the *privilege* to relate to God in prayer and only because of the indwelling Holy Spirit that we have the *power* to relate to God in prayer.

We never lose our standing, regardless of sin in our lives. When I feel like I can't go to God because of sin in my life that is when I need to run — not walk— into His presence. That is when I need to be there—when *we* need to be there. The privilege we have to be in the presence of God, to approach the throne of grace with confidence, has everything to do with Jesus Christ and what He did on our behalf because of God's love for us. It has nothing to do with our behavior. Our right to be in His presence at His throne has never been based in us, whether or not we were *good.* We just aren't good.

Love Matters

The church is the living, breathing representation of Jesus Christ. If we live (and continue to live) the Christian life apart from loving Him, individually and therefore collectively as the church, our message to the world is one of religion, and we are not true to our own testimony. Our words will say one thing and our lives another. We will still be saved, Christians, but our testimony will be without the light and the power of the gospel.

"If you do not repent, I will come to you and remove your lampstand from its place" (Revelation 2:4b).

Religion discounts the gospel. Religion teaches that we must do something in order to be loved, forgiven, and accepted by God. Jesus hates religion:

"Woe to you, teachers of the law and Pharisees, you hypocrites! You are like whitewashed tombs, which look beautiful on the outside but on the inside are full of dead men's bones and everything unclean" (Matthew 23:27).

Salvation is God's gift of grace to us, the proof of His love.

"For it is by grace you have been saved, through faith—and this not from yourselves. It is a gift of God—not by works, so that no one can boast" (Ephesians 2:8–9).

God will not force us to love Him. But we can know with certainty that He does love us. And we can know with certainty that He will never turn His back on us, regardless of the circumstances of our lives, or how we feel, or what appears to be true. We can know, absolutely, that God will never forsake us, because Jesus Christ was forsaken on our behalf! An amazing truth.

"About the ninth hour Jesus cried out in a loud voice, 'Eloi, Eloi, lama sabachthani?'—which means, 'My God, my God, why have you forsaken me?'" (Matthew 27:45–46).

God will never turn His back on us, because He turned His back on Jesus as Jesus became sin, so that in Him we might become the righteousness of God (2 Corinthians 5:21). We need never to turn our backs on God, our first love, because our first love has never withdrawn His heart from us. The measurement of God's love for us must be the cross!

"God demonstrates His own love for us in this: While we were still sinners, Christ died for us" (Romans 5:8).

Our witness to the watching world must be "Yes, life can be hard! But let me tell you about Jesus!" Our lives must reflect the glorious light and beauty of Jesus Christ, lovingly, authentically, worshipfully.

Beautiful

The river was long and well-defined; its parallel banks were thick with lush trees and plant life—but without color. In my entire field of vision, the only hint of colors I could see were varying shades of browns and tans, resembling an old-fashioned photograph negative. The temperature of the water and my own were exactly the same, creating the sensation that I was part of the river and it was a part of me. We were one. As my knees rested on the river floor, I was overwhelmed by peace—a perfect peace that is difficult to describe, a feeling of tranquility that I had never before experienced. *I was having a most unusual dream.*

Then, unexpectedly, I felt something irritating the inside corner of my left eye. I reached up with my left hand and removed it, and instantly I realized perfect vision. With absolute clarity, I was able to see what I had pulled from my eye: a sapphire, the brightest, most beautiful, deep blue sapphire I had ever seen. The blue color of the gem was a shade I had never seen anywhere on this earth. Contrasted against the drab colors of the sepia background, the sapphire was all the more stunning. Captivated by its brilliance, I couldn't look away; I didn't want to look away. I enjoyed it and held it close, moving it just beneath the crystal-clear surface of the water, carefully, with my hands. Its magnificence left me breathless and brought tears to my eyes. As the tears rolled down my face, they splashed into the water, becoming part of the river I was kneeling in. *Then I woke up,* still crying and roused to an extraordinary awareness of the presence of God and a powerful need to worship Him, quietly, personally.

I was convinced the dream was from the Lord. I spent the following three days deeply aware of His presence, prayerfully searching the Scriptures in the hope of finding significance to the thoughts I had had as I slept. I read and studied verses about dreams, sapphires, jewels, water, the river of life—anything and everything that was even remotely related to the lovely vision. But the Lord seemed silent. After much study and prayer, I became convinced in my spirit that the blue sapphire was a gift from the Lord and that something so beautiful must be offered *to* Him, because it was *from* Him. So that is what I did; I offered the sapphire to the Lord as an intentional act of worship *of Him*. Then the crying stopped. But the wonder, the fascination of the radiant blue sapphire, did not.

Several years later, when my daughter was deciding which college she would attend, our family attended a student-parent orientation at a university in New England. At the end of the information-packed day, there was a round table discussion that included a time of questions and answers for the prospective students and their parents. The professor who facilitated the conversation at our table held a PhD in astronomy.

The first question he was asked to answer was a personal inquiry: why did he choose to study astronomy? Without hesitation, he said that it was his fascination with the stars, specifically their colors.

The educator began to explain that when we see the stars through our unaided eyes, they pretty much all look the same—mostly white, with a few exceptions of slight color. He enthusiastically stated that when the stars are viewed through the lens of a powerful telescope, they can be seen in all of their vibrant colors: varying shades of reds and blues, greens, pinks, purples, oranges—his list went on and on. He said that the shades and the intensity of the colors were "out of this world," unlike any colors that can be found anywhere on this earth.

He was passionate about the stars and so excited to teach us about their beauty. I was excited too. At his mention of rare and unusual colors, my interest was more than piqued because of the dream that I had had years before about the stunning blue sapphire.

Then I asked the professor, "What is it that causes the stars to be so beautiful?" His answer began as one that was difficult to understand, rather scientific—something about a mixture of different gasses and the effects of varied temperatures—but then he said that the most important contributing factor to the stars' beauty was the light. He said that light is necessary to reflect the bright colors, and the more powerful the light, the more beautiful the colors become.

The Light of the World

I almost couldn't believe what I was hearing. *Light is necessary to reflect beauty.* My mind instantly raced through the pages of Scripture to where Jesus Himself remarks that He is the Light: "I am the Light of the world" (John 8:12).

I suddenly understood the essence of my dream. Jesus Christ, *the Light of the World,* reflects God's beautiful glory in our hearts through *His* story of our everyday lives. In the same way that the light brings beauty to the stars, Jesus brings beauty to the offering of our lives, our reasonable acts of worship.

The dream I had was a picture of everyday worship. The beautiful blue sapphire was a tear that symbolized my life, which through its offering became beautiful through the light of Jesus Christ. Jesus is the Light who reflects God's beautiful glory through all of our lives, *all who know Him personally.*

In that the Holy Spirit has removed the veil from our eyes, we are able to see God's radiant beauty not only in the starry heavens, but also in our own lives as we walk with Jesus Christ, *the radiance of God's glory,* in every trial, relationship, and situation. Abundantly! We are intended to enjoy Jesus richly, not to just get by in our circumstances, but to delight in our love relationship with Him through all of the many aspects of life.

The Holy Spirit has given us the spiritual eyesight we need, *the visual clarity,* to see the glory of God the Father through the face of His son, Jesus Christ, beginning at the cross of Calvary. In Him, we have been given the capacity to *realize* and to *reflect* God's glory. We are not the light; we are merely the light reflectors, imperfect clay pots, yet perfectly loved by God and entrusted with a profoundly beautiful treasure: the gospel message.

The light and life of Jesus is emitted in and through the circumstances of our lives when we *behold* the gospel—when we feast our eyes on its magnificence, subjecting ourselves to its power and purpose, becoming transformed by its supremacy from one level of glory to the next.

As I write this book and look back over my life, the Lord continues to use my own story with Him to encourage *me.* He has revealed to me the ongoing truth of Genesis 50:20: that although man intended to harm me, "God intended it for good to accomplish what is now being done, the saving of many lives" (Genesis 50:20b).

Beautiful. I am overwhelmed with a powerful love for our most awesome God. It is true that He has asked some hard things of me. Yes. However, He didn't ask the hardest thing of me. He did not ask me to pay for my own sin.

He did not ask the hardest thing of any of us—He did not ask any of us to pay for our own sin. Instead, He sent Jesus. Instead, Jesus came! He took our place! He paid our sin debt! He suffered God's wrath so that we wouldn't have to. He died our death! And He rose from the grave, *alive,* conquering sin, death, the grave, and hell. And because of that, when we believe on the Lord Jesus Christ for our salvation, we will have life *in* Him today and will rise to spend eternity *with* Him in heaven. That is love beyond comprehension. When I personally know these things about Jesus Christ, how can I not be compelled by His love for me? How can I not offer my life to Him? How can *we* not offer our lives to Him? I think that is a question worth pondering. Do you?

POSTLUDE

Proof

Unexpected and unrestrained, my quiet tears rolled liberally down my face, exposing the raw sadness that engulfed my aching heart. It was the morning after my sister's memorial service.

Without speaking a word, my mom reached over and gently covered my hand with her own. We rode together for many miles along the familiar river road, tenderly connected. No words were spoken; no words were necessary.

Oh, the power of a mother's touch.

The dynamic that amplified the power of my mom's touch can be encapsulated in just one word: forgiveness. God restored our once-lacking, *even non-existent,* relationship together to one of extraordinary shared love, all because of forgiveness.

Only because of Jesus, on that very sad day as my mom and I rode together along the river road, I was blessed to know *His* powerful love, love beyond comprehension, through the gentle placement of my mom's own aged hand as she rested it on mine; the *proof of redemption.*

Oh, the power of the Father's touch.

I stand in awe of the Lord's redemptive, healing power that has occurred in my life, founded first in Him and successively affecting every practical facet of my being—every memory, every relationship, and every situation, past, present and future—by faith.

I love being loved by my mom.

Look what God did!

A poem written by my mom, Jann Mattson
It is true—
how it was for years,
how it is today,
began with difficulty,
life for both of us,
the severity of life,
now the joy of life.

Life grew more,
more beautiful as we grew
closer and closer. The
hand of the Lord closed
the gap!

Maturity of the mind
seems best shown
in slow belief,
when it comes with
the Holy Spirit
guiding!

Unbelievable favor!
That was the host of
all we finally found.
The light of Christ
brought me to a
saving grace never
before known by me!

How hard it is to be a Christian!
Learning to be content with
what I had—hard lessons indeed.

Faith is the heart of my soul,
my mind, my deeds.

Faith takes us further
than I can see—
further than I was ever
able to comprehend.
Faith takes us further
than we can see alone!

Look what God did!

What about You?

If you are *not* a Christian but you sense that God is speaking to you about your sin and His forgiveness of sin, pray to Him, *talk to Him,* because Jesus died for you, too. Humble yourself; acknowledge your sin before Him and your need for a Savior. Receive His free gift of eternal life. And you will be forgiven and filled with the power and presence of God, the Holy Spirit. And you will spend eternity with God in heaven. Praise Him!

If you are a Christian and there is something or someone that God is asking you to forgive, just do it. Don't let someone else's sin against you become your own sin of unforgiveness against God. I know forgiving others is hard, but what is worth forfeiting intimacy with Jesus Christ? Nothing!

Or again, if there is something in your own life that until this very moment you have not accepted God's complete forgiveness for? Then accept it now. Just do it.

Why is realizing God's forgiveness so important? I mean, beyond the obvious "felt" reasons. Because when we *know* His forgiveness, *His love,* the Holy Spirit comes alive in us, and God's glory is reflected in and through our lives, drawing others to Himself—not to ourselves, but to Him. And that is what belonging to Jesus is all about.

The Gospel

One of the most astounding truths in the Word is that we were not an afterthought. Before the beginning of time, Jesus Christ was already in the picture—and always had been (2 Timothy 1:9). When Adam and Eve first sinned in the garden of Eden, God wasn't surprised. I promise you, the Father and the Son and the Holy Spirit were not looking down from heaven with disgust on their faces, saying "I can't believe they just went and ate that forbidden fruit. Now one of us is going to have to go down there and clean that mess up." No! Jesus Christ was always meant to be our Redeemer. We were always meant to belong to Him. We were *created* to be *His.*

Who Is Jesus Christ?

Jesus is Jesus, the Christ, the Lord God almighty (Hebrews 1:8), Son of God (Mark 1:1), Son of Man (Matthew 8:20), the Light of the World (John 8:12), the Bread from heaven (John 6:50), the Living Water (John 7:38), God in the flesh (Philippians 2:8), The Word of God (John 1:1), the Lamb of God (John 1:29), the Savior of the world (Philippians 3:20).

What Did He Do?

Jesus Christ gave His life for us so that we could live. His life wasn't taken from Him. He left heaven *willingly* to fulfill the perfect plan of the Father—to die on the cross for us (Hebrews 10:7). He reconciled us back into a right relationship with God (Romans 5:10); there was no other way. He gave His life for the sins of many (Hebrews 9:28) so that in Him we might become the righteousness of God (2 Corinthians 5:21). He died on the cross for us, sacrificially, receiving God's wrath for our sin (Romans 5:9). He *had* no sin of His own (2 Corinthians 5:21), but He took our place and paid our sin debt. We all sin; the Bible says that we do (Romans 6:23). It says that if we have even sinned one time, it is as if we have broken the whole law (James 2:10). It also says that the penalty for sin is death—eternal separation from God, experiencing His wrath as payment for our own sin (Romans 1:18; 6:23). Profoundly, God didn't just forgive us because He is a loving God. He satisfied *His own* requirement of *His own* law—that blood must be spilled for the remission of sin (Romans 8:3–4; Leviticus 17:11). The blood of Jesus Christ was the payment for our sin. When we believe and receive His righteousness in exchange for our sin, we are born again (1 Peter 2:24–25). Saved! Forgiven: covered with the perfect righteousness of Jesus Christ. Justified: declared not guilty, our sin washed away by His blood as though we have never sinned (Romans 3:22, Romans 5:9).

Why Did He do It?

He was motivated by His love for us and by our need for a Savior as sin separates us from God (John 3:16). Eternal life is God's gift to us (Romans 6:23). It's a free gift we receive by His grace and through our faith (Ephesians 2:8–9). He offers us this free gift because *He* is good, not because we are good. Jesus died for us because He loves us and wants a personal, intimate love relationship with us. God always had a plan of redemption for us—always. He wants to be in fellowship with us. The Trinity (the Father, Son, and Holy Spirit) have always enjoyed perfect fellowship together—apart from us. When we receive Christ, the Holy Spirit invites us to participate in that intimate fellowship with God. All we have to do is believe, accepting, by faith, what He has done on our behalf. Think about that! So much love!

John 3:16 sums it up: "God so loved the world that He gave His one and only Son, that whoever believes in Him shall not perish but have eternal life."

Everyone who *believes* in the Lord Jesus Christ *will* have eternal life with God that begins now, this side of heaven. Everyone who does *not believe* does not have eternal life with God and will in fact be separated from God for all of eternity (John 3:36).

It absolutely breaks my heart to think that there may be someone reading this book who is living and perhaps even suffering apart from Jesus. Please, again, if as you read the gospel (above), you feel a stirring in your heart, call upon the name of the Lord Jesus Christ, and you will be saved! *Believe!* Know that Jesus loves you! Believe that through the gospel—the death, burial, and resurrection of Jesus Christ—you have been forgiven: purchased to live *in* Christ during this lifetime and forever *with* Him throughout eternity (Galatians 2:20; 5:1; John 3:16)!

"I tell you the truth, whoever hears my word and believes Him who sent me has eternal life and will not be condemned; he has crossed over from death to life" (John 5:24).

I am honored to belong to Jesus, bought and paid for; privileged to know and love Him personally, through the beautiful gospel. I will forever be *His.*

Printed in the United States
By Bookmasters